Simple 1-2-3™

Entertaining

Publications International, Ltd.

Favorite Brand Name Recipes at www.fbnr.com

Microwave Cooking: Microwave ovens vary in wattage. Use the cooking times as guidelines and check for doneness before adding more time.

Preparation/Cooking Times: Preparation times are based on the approximate amount of time required to assemble the recipe before cooking, baking, chilling or serving. These times include preparation steps such as measuring, chopping and mixing. The fact that some preparations and cooking can be done simultaneously is taken into account. Preparation of optional ingredients and serving suggestions is not included.

Contents

Bits & Bites

Pizzette with Basil

1 can (6 ounces)
CONTADINA® Italian
Paste with Italian
Seasonings
2 tablespoons softened
cream cheese
2 tablespoons chopped
fresh basil *or*
2 teaspoons dried
basil leaves
1 loaf (1 pound) Italian
bread, sliced ¼ inch
thick
8 ounces mozzarella
cheese, thinly sliced
Whole fresh basil leaves
(optional)
Freshly ground black
pepper (optional)

1. Combine tomato paste, cream cheese and chopped basil in small bowl.

2. Toast bread slices on *ungreased* baking sheet under broiler, 6 to 8 inches from heat, until lightly browned on both sides, turning after 1 minute; remove from broiler.

3. Spread 2 teaspoons tomato mixture onto each toasted bread slice; top with 1 slice (about ¼ ounce) mozzarella cheese.

4. Broil 6 to 8 inches from heat for 1 to 2 minutes or until cheese begins to melt. Top with whole basil leaves and pepper, if desired.

Makes about 30 pizzas

Prep Time: *7 minutes*
Cook Time: *10 minutes*

Crab Canapés

⅔ cup fat-free cream cheese, softened
2 teaspoons lemon juice
1 teaspoon hot pepper sauce
1 package (8 ounces) imitation crabmeat or lobster, flaked
⅓ cup chopped red bell pepper
2 green onions, sliced (about ¼ cup)
64 cucumber slices (about 2½ medium cucumbers, cut into ⅜-inch-thick slices) or melba toast rounds
Fresh parsley for garnish (optional)

1. Combine cream cheese, lemon juice and hot pepper sauce in medium bowl; mix well.

2. Stir in crabmeat, bell pepper and green onions; cover. Chill until ready to serve.

3. When ready to serve, spoon 1½ teaspoons crabmeat mixture onto each cucumber slice. Place on serving plate; garnish with parsley, if desired.

Makes 16 servings

Tip: To allow flavors to blend, chill crab mixture at least 1 hour before spreading onto cucumbers or melba toast rounds.

Bits & Bites

Fruit Antipasto Platter

• Arrange fruit, onion, cheese and artichoke hearts on lettuce-lined platter; serve with dressing. Garnish, if desired. *Makes 10 servings*

Tip: Make this scrumptious dish even lighter by substituting fat-free Italian salad dressing for the high-calorie regular dressing.

2 cups fresh DOLE® Tropical Gold® Pineapple, cut into wedges
2 medium, firm DOLE® Bananas, sliced diagonally
2 oranges, peeled and sliced
½ cup thinly sliced DOLE® Red Onion
½ pound low fat sharp Cheddar cheese, cut into 1-inch cubes
2 jars (6 ounces each) marinated artichoke hearts, drained and halved
DOLE® Green or Red Leaf Lettuce
½ cup Italian salad dressing

Bits & Bites

Apricot BBQ Glazed Shrimp and Bacon

1 can (8 ounces) sliced
    water chestnuts,
    drained
36 medium raw shrimp,
    peeled and deveined
    (about 1¼ pounds)
9 slices bacon, each cut
    into 4 pieces
⅓ cup barbecue sauce
⅓ cup apricot fruit spread
1 tablespoon grated fresh
    ginger
1 tablespoon cider vinegar
⅛ teaspoon red pepper
    flakes

1. Preheat broiler. Place 1 water chestnut slice on top of each shrimp. Wrap 1 piece of bacon around shrimp and secure with wooden toothpick. Repeat with remaining water chestnuts, shrimp and bacon.

2. Line broiler pan with foil; insert broiler rack. Coat broiler rack with nonstick cooking spray. Place shrimp on rack.

3. Combine remaining ingredients in small bowl. Brush sauce evenly over shrimp. Broil 2 minutes; turn. Baste and broil 2 minutes more; turn again. Baste and broil 1 minute more or until edges of bacon begin to brown.

Makes 36 appetizers

Bits & Bites

Caesar Salad in Crouton Cups

Preheat oven to 350°F. Spray 12-muffin pan with CRISCO® Cooking Spray. Trim crusts off bread; spray both sides of bread with CRISCO® Cooking Spray.

In a small bowl, mix together the garlic salt, thyme, rosemary and cracked pepper. Lightly sprinkle mixture over both sides of bread.

Use a rolling pin to slightly flatten bread and embed the spice mixture. Press each slice into a muffin cup, allowing edges to hang over cup.

Bake for 12 to 15 minutes or until golden brown and crisp. Remove from oven and cool. Toss lettuce and green onions with dressing. Spoon salad into Crouton Cups. Garnish with shredded Parmesan and green onion slices. Serve immediately.   *Makes 12 appetizer servings*

Prep Time: *10 minutes*
Bake Time: *12 to 15 minutes*

CRISCO® Butter Flavor No-Stick Cooking Spray
12 slices white bread
1 teaspoon garlic salt
1 teaspoon thyme
1 teaspoon rosemary
½ teaspoon cracked pepper
4 cups romaine lettuce, finely sliced into ⅛-inch strips
2 green onions, thinly sliced, plus additional for garnish
Purchased Caesar dressing, to taste
Shredded Parmesan cheese

Bits & Bites

Turkey Meatballs in Cranberry-Barbecue Sauce

1 can (16 ounces) jellied
    cranberry sauce
½ cup barbecue sauce
1 egg white
1 pound 93% lean ground
    turkey
1 green onion, sliced
2 teaspoons grated orange
    peel
1 teaspoon soy sauce
¼ teaspoon black pepper
⅛ teaspoon ground red
    pepper (optional)
    Nonstick cooking spray

Slow Cooker Directions

1. Combine cranberry sauce and barbecue sauce in slow cooker. Cover; cook on HIGH 20 to 30 minutes or until cranberry sauce is melted and mixture is hot.

2. Meanwhile, place egg white in medium bowl; beat lightly. Add turkey, green onion, orange peel, soy sauce, black pepper and ground red pepper, if desired; mix until well blended. Shape into 24 balls.

3. Spray large nonstick skillet with cooking spray. Add meatballs to skillet; cook over medium heat 8 to 10 minutes or until meatballs are no longer pink in center, carefully turning occasionally to brown evenly. Add to heated sauce in slow cooker; stir gently to coat. Reduce heat to LOW. Cover; cook 3 hours. Transfer meatballs to serving plate; garnish, if desired.

Makes 12 servings

Spicy Thai Satay Dip

1. Combine all ingredients in large bowl. Cover and refrigerate.
2. Serve with grilled meats, vegetables or chips.

Makes 4 (¼-cup) servings

Prep Time: *10 minutes*

⅓ cup peanut butter
⅓ cup *French's*® Honey Dijon Mustard
⅓ cup fat-free chicken broth
1 tablespoon chopped peeled fresh ginger
1 tablespoon grated orange peel
1 tablespoon honey
1 tablespoon *Frank's*® *RedHot*® Original Cayenne Pepper Sauce
1 tablespoon teriyaki sauce
2 cloves garlic, minced

·11·

Bits & Bites

Tomato and Caper Crostini

1 French roll (about
1½ ounces), cut
into 8 slices
2 plum tomatoes (about
4 ounces), finely
chopped
1½ tablespoons capers
1½ teaspoons dried basil
1 teaspoon extra-virgin
olive oil
¼ cup (1 ounce) crumbled
feta (any variety,
preferably sun-dried
tomato and basil)

1. Preheat oven to 350°F.

2. Place bread slices on ungreased baking sheet in single layer. Bake 15 minutes or just until golden brown. Cool completely.

3. Meanwhile, combine tomatoes, capers, basil and oil in small bowl. Just before serving, spoon tomato mixture onto each bread slice; sprinkle with cheese.

Makes 2 servings

Easy Cheese Fondue

1. In medium bowl, coat cheese with cornstarch; set aside. Rub inside of ceramic fondue pot or heavy saucepan with garlic; discard garlic. Bring wine to gentle simmer over medium heat in prepared pot.

2. Gradually stir in cheese to ensure smooth fondue. Once smooth, stir in brandy, if desired. Garnish with nutmeg and pepper.

3. Serve with bite-sized chunks of French bread, broccoli, cauliflower, tart apples or pears. Spear with fondue forks or wooden skewers.

Makes 1¼ cups

1 pound low-sodium Swiss cheese (Gruyère, Emmentaler or combination of both), cubed, divided
2 tablespoons cornstarch
1 garlic clove, crushed
1 cup HOLLAND HOUSE® White or White with Lemon Cooking Wine
1 tablespoon kirsch or cherry brandy (optional)
Pinch nutmeg
Ground black pepper

Wisconsin Edam and Beer Spread

4 cups shredded Wisconsin Edam Cheese*

¾ cup butter, cubed and softened

2 tablespoons snipped fresh chives

2 teaspoons Dijon mustard

½ cup amber ale or dark beer, at room temperature

Cocktail rye or pumpernickel bread slices

*Wisconsin Gouda can be substituted for Edam.

In large bowl, place shredded cheese, butter, chives and mustard; mix with spoon until blended. Stir in beer until blended. Chill until serving time. Serve as spread with cocktail bread.

Makes 4 cups

Variation: Cut ⅕ from the top of a 2-pound Wisconsin Edam Cheese ball. With a butter curler or melon baller, remove the cheese from the center of the ball, leaving a ½-inch-thick shell. Shred enough of the cheese removed from the ball to measure 4 cups. Reserve any remaining cheese for another use. Follow directions given above. Spoon spread into the hollowed-out cheese ball; reserve remaining spread for refills. Chill until serving time.

*Favorite recipe from **Wisconsin Milk Marketing Board***

Skewered Antipasto

Drain oil from tomatoes into medium bowl. Place tomatoes in small bowl; set aside. Cut potatoes into 1-inch cubes. Add potatoes, vegetables, tortellini, chives and rosemary to oil in medium bowl. Stir to coat with oil; cover and marinate 1 hour at room temperature. To assemble, alternately thread tomatoes, potatoes, vegetables and tortellini onto 6-inch skewers.

Makes 12 to 14 skewers

1 jar (8 ounces) SONOMA® marinated dried tomatoes
1 pound (3 medium) new potatoes, cooked until tender
2 cups bite-sized vegetable pieces (such as celery, bell peppers, radishes, carrots, cucumber and green onions)
1 cup drained cooked egg tortellini and/or spinach tortellini
1 tablespoon chopped fresh chives *or* 1 teaspoon dried chives
1 tablespoon chopped fresh rosemary *or* 1 teaspoon dried rosemary

Marinated Roasted Pepper Tapas

1 large red bell pepper
1 large yellow bell pepper
3 tablespoons olive oil
1 tablespoon capers, rinsed
    and drained
1 tablespoon sherry wine
    vinegar or white wine
    vinegar
1 teaspoon sugar
1 clove garlic, sliced
½ teaspoon cumin seeds
1 loaf French bread, sliced

1. Cover broiler pan with foil. Preheat broiler. Place peppers on foil. Broil 4 inches from heat 15 to 20 minutes or until blackened on all sides, turning peppers every 5 minutes with tongs. Remove peppers to paper bag for 30 minutes. Meanwhile, place oil, capers, vinegar, sugar, garlic and cumin seeds in small bowl. Whisk until combined.

2. Peel, core and seed peppers; cut into 1-inch diamond- or square-shaped pieces. Place in resealable food storage bag. Pour oil mixture over peppers. Cover and refrigerate at least 2 hours or overnight, turning occasionally. Bring to room temperature before serving.

3. Toast bread slices, if desired. Arrange pepper mixture on top of bread slices.

Makes 4 to 6 servings

Cheesy Potato Skin Appetizers

1. Preheat oven to 425°F. Scrub potatoes; pierce several times with fork. Bake 45 minutes or until soft. Cool.

2. Split each potato crosswise into halves. Scoop out potato with spoon, leaving ¼-inch-thick shell. (Reserve potato pulp for another use, if desired.) Place potato skins on baking sheet; spray lightly with cooking spray. Preheat broiler. Broil potato skins 6 inches from heat 5 minutes or until lightly browned and crisp.

3. *Reduce oven temperature to 350°F.* Combine cream cheese and sour cream in small bowl; stir until well blended. Divide mixture among potato skins; spread to cover. Top with salsa, cheese and olives, if desired. Bake 15 minutes or until heated through. Sprinkle with cilantro. *Makes 10 servings*

5 potatoes (4 to 5 ounces each)
Butter-flavored nonstick cooking spray
½ package (4 ounces) cream cheese
2 tablespoons sour cream
⅔ cup prepared salsa
⅓ cup shredded sharp Cheddar cheese
2 tablespoons sliced ripe olives (optional)
¼ cup minced fresh cilantro

Hidden Valley® Torta

2 packages (8 ounces each) cream cheese
1 packet (1 ounce) HIDDEN VALLEY® The Original Ranch® Salad Dressing & Seasoning Mix
1 jar (6 ounces) marinated artichoke hearts, drained and chopped
⅓ cup roasted red peppers, drained and chopped
3 tablespoons minced fresh parsley

Beat cream cheese and salad dressing & seasoning mix together in a medium bowl. In a separate bowl, stir together artichokes, peppers and parsley. In a 3-cup bowl lined with plastic wrap, alternate layers of cream cheese and vegetable mixtures, beginning and ending with a cheese layer.

Chill 4 hours or overnight. Invert onto plate; remove plastic wrap. Garnish with additional minced fresh parley and roasted red peppers, if desired. Serve with crackers.

Makes 10 to 12 servings

Summer Sausage Dippers

Secure 1 piece cheese and 1 olive onto 1 Summer Sausage slice with frilled toothpick; repeat with remaining cheese, olives and sausage. Arrange on platter. Cover and refrigerate until ready to serve. For dipping sauce, stir ketchup, jam, vinegar and Worcestershire sauce in small saucepan; heat over medium-low heat until warm and smooth. Serve sausage dippers with sauce.

Makes 8 servings

5 ounces sharp Cheddar cheese, cut into 1×½-inch chunks
32 pimiento-stuffed green olives
1 (9-ounce) HILLSHIRE FARM® Summer Sausage, cut into 32 thick half-moon slices
1 cup ketchup
½ cup apricot jam or preserves
1 tablespoon cider vinegar
2 teaspoons Worcestershire sauce

Bits & Bites

Sausage-Stuffed Mushrooms

¼ pound uncooked Italian turkey sausage
2 tablespoons plain dry bread crumbs
4 medium portobello mushroom caps
1 tablespoon olive oil
¼ cup (1 ounce) shredded Asiago cheese

1. Preheat oven or toaster oven to 325°F. Remove sausage from casing. Crumble sausage into small skillet. Cook over medium-high heat until lightly browned, stirring frequently; drain fat. Remove from heat and stir in bread crumbs.

2. Brush both sides of mushroom caps lightly with oil. Spoon sausage stuffing into caps, dividing evenly among mushrooms.

3. Place mushrooms, stuffing side up, on toaster oven tray. Sprinkle 1 tablespoon cheese over each mushroom. Bake 15 minutes or until cheese melts and mushrooms are tender.

Makes 4 servings

Italian-Topped Garlic Bread

Preheat oven to 325°F. Crumble and cook sausage in medium skillet until browned. Drain off any drippings. Cut bread into 1-inch slices. Combine butter and garlic in small bowl; brush bread slices with mixture. Arrange on ungreased baking sheet. Combine mozzarella cheese, tomatoes, mushrooms, Parmesan cheese and sausage; spread on bread slices. Bake 10 to 12 minutes or until cheese is melted and golden brown. Serve warm. Refrigerate leftovers.

Makes about 10 appetizer servings

1 pound **BOB EVANS®** **Italian Roll Sausage**
1 (1-pound) loaf crusty **Italian bread**
½ **cup butter, melted**
2 **teaspoons minced garlic**
2 **cups (8 ounces) shredded mozzarella cheese**
2 **cups diced tomatoes**
8 **ounces fresh mushrooms, sliced**
3 **tablespoons grated Parmesan cheese**

Toasted Pesto Rounds

¼ cup thinly sliced fresh basil or chopped fresh dill

¼ cup grated Parmesan cheese

3 tablespoons mayonnaise

1 medium clove garlic, minced

12 slices French bread, each about ¼ inch thick

1 tablespoon plus 1 teaspoon chopped fresh tomato

1 green onion, sliced
Black pepper

1. Preheat broiler. Combine basil, cheese, mayonnaise and garlic in small bowl; mix well.

2. Arrange bread slices in single layer on large ungreased nonstick baking sheet or broiler pan. Broil 6 to 8 inches from heat 30 to 45 seconds or until bread slices are lightly toasted.

3. Turn bread slices over; spread evenly with basil mixture. Broil 1 minute or until lightly browned. Top evenly with tomato and green onion. Season to taste with pepper. *Makes 12 servings*

Peppery Brie en Croûte

Preheat oven to 375°F. Work crescent roll dough into thin circle large enough to completely wrap cheese. Place cheese in center of dough circle. Prick top of cheese several times with fork. Slowly pour 1 tablespoon TABASCO® Green Pepper Sauce over top of cheese. Let stand briefly for sauce to sink in.

Add remaining 1 tablespoon TABASCO® Green Pepper Sauce, pricking cheese several more times with fork. (Some sauce will run over side of cheese.) Bring edges of dough over top of cheese, working it together to completely cover cheese. Brush edges with beaten egg and seal. Bake about 10 minutes, following directions on crescent roll package. (Do not overbake, as cheese will run.) Serve immediately with crackers.   *Makes 8 to 10 servings*

2 (4-ounce) packages crescent roll dough
1 (8-ounce) wheel Brie cheese
2 tablespoons TABASCO® brand Green Pepper Sauce
1 egg, beaten
Crackers

Clams Casino

8 slices bacon, diced
1 medium onion, chopped
1 green bell pepper, chopped
1 red bell pepper, chopped
1 cup butter or margarine, softened
¼ cup lemon juice
⅛ teaspoon ground red pepper
24 medium cherrystone clams, shucked and chopped (reserve 3 tablespoons clam juice)
¼ cup Italian-seasoned dry bread crumbs

1. Cook and stir bacon in large skillet over medium-high heat until crisp. Remove with slotted spoon; drain on paper towels. Set bacon aside.

2. Preheat oven to 350°F. Discard all but 1 tablespoon bacon drippings from skillet. Cook and stir onion and bell peppers in same skillet over medium-high heat until onion is tender but not brown. Let stand at room temperature to cool slightly.

3. Combine butter and lemon juice in small bowl; mix well. Add bacon, onion-pepper mixture and ground red pepper. Combine clams, reserved clam juice and bread crumbs in another small bowl. Place clam shells on baking sheets. Fill clam shells half full with clam mixture and top with 1 tablespoon butter mixture.* Bake 20 minutes or until lightly browned. Garnish as desired.

Makes about 16 servings

Clams may be frozen at this point. When ready to serve, place frozen clams on baking sheet; bake in preheated 350°F oven 20 to 25 minutes.

Angelic Deviled Eggs

1. Place eggs in medium saucepan; add enough water to cover. Bring to a boil over medium heat. Remove from heat; cover. Let stand 15 minutes. Drain. Add cold water to eggs in saucepan; let stand until eggs are cool. Drain. Remove shells from eggs; discard shells.

2. Slice eggs lengthwise in half. Remove yolks, reserving 3 yolk halves. Discard remaining yolks or reserve for another use. Place egg whites, cut sides up, on serving plate; cover with plastic wrap. Refrigerate while preparing filling.

3. Combine cottage cheese, dressing, mustard and reserved yolk halves in mini food processor; cover and process until smooth. (Or, place in small bowl and mash with fork until well blended.) Transfer cottage cheese mixture to small bowl; stir in chives and pimiento. Spoon into egg whites. Cover and chill at least 1 hour. Garnish, if desired. *Makes 12 servings*

6 eggs
¼ cup cottage cheese
3 tablespoons prepared ranch dressing
2 teaspoons Dijon mustard
2 tablespoons minced fresh chives or dill
1 tablespoon well-drained diced pimiento or roasted red pepper

Bits & Bites

Chunky Hawaiian Spread

1 package (3 ounces) light
    cream cheese, softened
½ cup fat free or light sour
    cream
1 can (8 ounces) DOLE®
    Crushed Pineapple,
    well drained
¼ cup mango chutney*
    Low fat crackers

*If there are large pieces of fruit in
chutney, cut them into small pieces.

• Beat cream cheese, sour cream, crushed pineapple and chutney in bowl until blended. Cover and chill 1 hour or overnight. Serve with crackers. Refrigerate any leftover spread in airtight container for up to 1 week.

Makes 2½ cups

Bits & Bites

Spicy Marinated Shrimp

Combine all ingredients except shrimp in large bowl. Add shrimp and toss to coat. Cover and refrigerate 4 to 6 hours or overnight. Transfer shrimp mixture to serving bowl and serve with toothpicks.   *Makes 30 to 40 shrimp*

1 green onion, finely chopped
2 tablespoons olive oil
2 tablespoons fresh lemon juice
2 tablespoons prepared horseradish
2 tablespoons ketchup
1 tablespoon finely chopped chives
1 teaspoon TABASCO® brand Pepper Sauce
1 teaspoon Dijon mustard
1 clove garlic, minced
Salt to taste
2 pounds medium shrimp, cooked, peeled and deveined

Dips & Dunks

Smoky Eggplant Dip

1 large eggplant (about
  1 pound)
¼ cup olive oil
3 tablespoons *Frank's®
  RedHot®* Original
  Cayenne Pepper Sauce
2 tablespoons peanut
  butter or tahini paste
1 tablespoon lemon juice
2 cloves garlic, minced
¾ teaspoon salt
½ teaspoon ground cumin
  Spicy Pita Chips (recipe
  follows)

1. Prepare grill. Place eggplant on oiled grid. Grill over hot coals 15 minutes or until soft and skin is charred, turning often. Remove from grill; cool until easy enough to handle.

2. Peel skin from eggplant with paring knife; discard. Coarsely chop eggplant. Place in strainer or kitchen towel. Press out excess liquid.

3. Place eggplant in food processor; add oil, *Frank's RedHot* Sauce, peanut butter, lemon juice, garlic, salt and cumin. Cover; process until mixture is very smooth. Remove eggplant mixture to bowl. Cover; refrigerate until chilled. Serve with Spicy Pita Chips.   *Makes 1½ cups dip*

Spicy Pita Chips: Split 4 pita bread rounds in half lengthwise. Combine ½ cup olive oil, ¼ cup *Frank's RedHot* Sauce and 1 tablespoon minced garlic in small bowl. Brush mixture on both sides of pitas. Place pitas on grid. Grill over medium coals about 5 minutes or until crispy, turning once. Cut pitas into triangles.

Prep Time: 30 minutes
Cook Time: 20 minutes
Chill Time: 30 minutes

2 very ripe avocados,
    seeded, peeled and
    mashed
1 can (4 ounces) ORTEGA®
    Diced Green Chiles
2 large green onions,
    chopped
2 tablespoons olive oil
1 teaspoon lime juice
1 clove garlic, finely
    chopped
¼ teaspoon salt
    Tortilla chips

Ortega® Green Chile Guacamole

COMBINE avocados, chiles, green onions, olive oil, lime juice, garlic and salt in medium bowl. Cover; refrigerate for at least 1 hour. Serve with chips.

Makes 2 cups

Tip: This all-time favorite dip can be served with tacos, burritos, tamales or chimichangas. Or combine it with ORTEGA® Salsa for a scrumptious spicy salad dressing.

Dips & Dunks

Cucumber-Dill Dip

1. Lightly salt cucumber in small bowl; toss. Refrigerate 1 hour. Drain cucumber; dry on paper towels. Return cucumbers to bowl and add onions. Set aside.

2. Place cream cheese, yogurt and 2 tablespoons fresh dill in food processor or blender container; cover and process until smooth. Stir into cucumber mixture. Cover; refrigerate 1 hour.

3. Spoon dip into serving bowl; garnish with fresh dill sprig, if desired.

Makes about 2 cups dip

Salt
1 cucumber, peeled, seeded and finely chopped
6 green onions (white parts only), chopped
1 package (3 ounces) cream cheese
1 cup plain yogurt
2 tablespoons fresh dill *or* 1 tablespoon dried dill weed
Fresh dill sprig for garnish (optional)

7-Layer Ranch Dip

1 envelope LIPTON®
    RECIPE SECRETS®
    Ranch Soup Mix
1 container (16 ounces)
    sour cream
1 cup shredded lettuce
1 medium tomato,
    chopped (about 1 cup)
1 can (2.25 ounces) sliced
    pitted ripe olives,
    drained
¼ cup chopped red onion
1 can (4.5 ounces)
    chopped green chilies,
    drained
1 cup shredded Cheddar
    cheese (about
    4 ounces)

1. In 2-quart shallow dish, combine soup mix and sour cream.

2. Evenly layer remaining ingredients, ending with cheese. Chill, if desired. Serve with tortilla chips. *Makes 7 cups dip*

Prep Time: *15 minutes*

Dips & Dunks

Dreamy Orange Cheesecake Dip

1. Combine cream cheese, marmalade and vanilla in small bowl; mix well. Garnish with orange peel and mint leaves, if desired.

2. Serve with fruit dippers.

Makes 12 servings

Note: Dip can be prepared ahead of time. Store, covered, in refrigerator for up to 2 days.

1 package (8 ounces) cream cheese, softened
½ cup orange marmalade
½ teaspoon vanilla
  Grated orange peel (optional)
  Mint leaves (optional)
2 cups whole strawberries
2 cups cantaloupe chunks
2 cups apple slices

Hidden Valley® Bacon-Cheddar Ranch Dip

1 container (16 ounces) sour cream (2 cups)

1 packet (1 ounce) HIDDEN VALLEY® The Original Ranch® Dips Mix

1 cup (4 ounces) shredded Cheddar cheese

¼ cup crisp-cooked, crumbled bacon*

Potato chips or corn chips, for dipping

*Bacon pieces can be used.

Combine sour cream and dips mix. Stir in cheese and bacon. Garnish as desired. Chill at least 1 hour. Serve with chips.   *Makes about 3 cups*

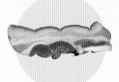

Olive Tapenade Dip

1. Place all ingredients in food processor. Process until puréed.

2. Transfer to serving bowl. Garnish as desired.

3. Serve with vegetable crudités or pita chips.   *Makes 4 (¼-cup) servings*

Tip: To pit olives, place them in a plastic bag and gently tap them with a wooden mallet or rolling pin until they split open. Remove the pits.

Prep Time: *10 minutes*

**1½ cups (10-ounce jar)
   pitted kalamata olives
3 tablespoons olive oil
3 tablespoons *French's*®
   Bold n' Spicy Brown
   Mustard
1 tablespoon minced fresh
   rosemary leaves *or*
1 teaspoon dried
   rosemary leaves
1 teaspoon minced garlic**

Pizza Fondue

½ pound Italian sausage
1 cup chopped onion
2 jars (26 ounces each)
    meatless pasta sauce
¼ pound thinly sliced ham,
    finely chopped
1 package (3 ounces) sliced
    pepperoni, finely
    chopped
¼ teaspoon red pepper
    flakes
1 pound mozzarella
    cheese, cut into ¾-inch
    cubes
1 loaf Italian or French
    bread, cut into 1-inch
    cubes

Slow Cooker Directions

1. Remove sausage from casing. Crumble sausage into large skillet. Add onion. Cook sausage and onion, stirring occasionally, until sausage is browned. Drain fat.

2. Transfer sausage mixture to slow cooker. Stir in pasta sauce, ham, pepperoni and red pepper flakes. Cover; cook on LOW 3 to 4 hours.

3. Serve fondue with cheese and bread cubes. *Makes 20 to 25 servings*

Three Bean Salsa

In 12-inch skillet, blend savory herb with garlic soup mix with water. Bring to a boil over high heat; stir in tomato. Reduce heat to low and simmer 3 minutes. Stir in beans and simmer 3 minutes or until heated through. Stir in vinegar. Garnish, if desired, with chopped fresh parsley or cilantro.

Makes about 4 cups salsa

Serving Suggestion: Serve as a side dish or as a topping to grilled poultry, beef, lamb or pork.

1 envelope LIPTON®
   RECIPE SECRETS®
   Savory Herb with
   Garlic Soup Mix
½ cup water
1 large tomato, chopped
1 cup drained canned
   cannellini or red
   kidney beans
1 cup drained canned
   black or pinto beans
1 cup drained canned
   chick-peas or garbanzo
   beans
2 teaspoons white wine
   vinegar (optional)

Special Dark® Fudge Fondue

2 cups (12-ounce package)
   HERSHEY'S SPECIAL
   DARK® Chocolate
   Chips
½ cup light cream
2 teaspoons vanilla extract
   Assorted fondue dippers
   such as marshmallows,
   cherries, grapes,
   mandarin orange
   segments, pineapple
   chunks, strawberries,
   slices of other fresh
   fruits, small pieces of
   cake, or small
   brownies

1. Place chocolate chips and light cream in medium microwave-safe bowl. Microwave on HIGH (100%) 1 minute or just until chips are melted and mixture is smooth when stirred. Stir in vanilla.

2. Pour into fondue pot or chafing dish; serve warm with fondue dippers. If mixture thickens, stir in additional light cream, one tablespoon at a time. Refrigerate leftover fondue.   *Makes 1½ cups fondue*

Stovetop Directions: Combine chocolate chips and light cream in medium heavy saucepan. Cook over low heat, stirring constantly, until chips are melted and mixture is hot. Stir in vanilla, and continue as in Step 2 above.

The Famous Lipton® California Dip

1. In medium bowl, blend all ingredients; chill at least 2 hours.

2. Serve with your favorite dippers.   *Makes about 2 cups dip*

Tip: For a creamier dip, add more sour cream.

Sensational Spinach Dip: Add 1 package (10 ounces) frozen chopped spinach, thawed and squeezed dry.

California Seafood Dip: Add 1 cup finely chopped cooked clams, crabmeat or shrimp, ¼ cup chili sauce and 1 tablespoon horseradish.

California Bacon Dip: Add ⅓ cup crumbled cooked bacon or bacon bits.

California Blue Cheese Dip: Add ¼ pound crumbled blue cheese and ¼ cup finely chopped walnuts.

**1 envelope LIPTON®
RECIPE SECRETS®
Onion Soup Mix
1 container (16 ounces)
regular or light sour
cream**

Beer Cheese Dip

2 cups shredded Cheddar
   cheese
2 packages (8 ounces each)
   cream cheese, softened
1 packet (1 ounce)
   HIDDEN VALLEY® The
   Original Ranch® Salad
   Dressing & Seasoning
   Mix
½ to ¾ cup beer
   Chopped green onion
   and additional
   Cheddar cheese
   for garnish

In medium bowl, combine 2 cups Cheddar cheese, cream cheese and salad dressing & seasoning mix. Gradually stir in beer until mixture is to desired consistency. Garnish with green onion and additional Cheddar cheese. Serve with pretzels or assorted fresh vegetables, if desired.   *Makes about 3 cups*

Dips & Dunks

Hot Black Bean Dip

1. Place beans in medium bowl; mash with fork until smooth. Transfer to small heavy saucepan. Stir in tomatoes, chipotle and oregano. Cook over medium heat 5 minutes or until heated through, stirring occasionally.

2. Remove saucepan from heat. Add cheese; stir constantly until cheese melts.

3. Transfer bean dip to serving bowl. Serve hot with tortilla chips.

Makes 8 servings

1 can (about 15 ounces) black beans, rinsed and drained
1 can (14½ ounces) whole peeled tomatoes, drained and chopped
1 canned chipotle pepper in adobo sauce,* drained and minced
1 teaspoon dried oregano
1 cup (4 ounces) shredded Cheddar cheese
Baked tortilla chips

Chipotle peppers can sting and irritate the skin. Wear rubber gloves when handling peppers and do not touch eyes.

Golden Artichoke Dip

1 envelope LIPTON®
 RECIPE SECRETS®
 Golden Onion Soup
 Mix*
1 can (14 ounces)
 artichoke hearts,
 drained and chopped
1 cup HELLMANN'S® or
 BEST FOODS® Real
 Mayonnaise
1 container (8 ounces) sour
 cream
1 cup shredded Swiss or
 mozzarella cheese
 (about 4 ounces)

*Also terrific with LIPTON® RECIPE
SECRETS® Savory Herb with Garlic
or Onion Soup Mix.

1. Preheat oven to 350°F. In 1-quart casserole, combine all ingredients.

2. Bake 30 minutes or until heated through.

3. Serve with your favorite dippers. *Makes 3 cups dip*

Variation: For a cold artichoke dip, omit Swiss cheese. Stir in, if desired, ¼ cup grated Parmesan cheese. Do not bake.

Tip: For a quick party fix or anytime treat, try these CLASSIC LIPTON® DIPS: Combine 1 envelope Lipton® Recipe Secrets® Onion, Ranch, Savory Herb with Garlic, Onion Mushroom, Beefy Onion or Vegetable Soup Mix with 1 container (16 ounces) sour cream. Chill and serve with your favorite dippers.

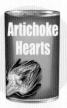

Dips & Dunks

Garlic Bean Dip

1. Place garlic in food processor; cover and process until minced.

2. Add beans, olives, lemon juice and cumin; cover and process until well blended but not completely smooth.

3. Serve with vegetables and crackers. Garnish, if desired.

Makes 12 servings (about 1½ cups dip)

Tip: To save time, buy cut-up fresh vegetables such as carrots and celery from the salad bar or produce section of the supermarket.

4 cloves garlic
1 can (about 15 ounces) black or pinto beans, rinsed and drained
¼ cup pimiento-stuffed green olives
4½ teaspoons lemon juice
½ teaspoon ground cumin
Assorted fresh vegetables and crackers

Dips & Dunks

2 large avocados, pitted and peeled
¼ cup finely chopped tomato
2 tablespoons grated onion with juice
2 tablespoons lime juice or lemon juice
½ teaspoon salt
¼ teaspoon hot pepper sauce
Black pepper
Additional chopped tomato (optional)

Guacamole

1. Place avocados in medium bowl; mash coarsely with fork. Stir in ¼ cup tomato, onion with juice, lime juice, salt and hot pepper sauce; mix well. Add black pepper to taste.

2. Spoon into serving container. Serve immediately, or cover and refrigerate up to 2 hours.

3. Garnish with additional chopped tomato, if desired.   *Makes 2 cups*

Tip: To ripen hard avocados, store them in a loosely closed paper bag at room temperature for 2 to 4 days.

Original Ranch® Spinach Dip

Stir together sour cream, spinach, water chestnuts and salad dressing & seasoning mix. Chill 30 minutes. Just before serving, cut top off bread and remove center, reserving firm bread pieces. Fill bread bowl with dip. Cut reserved bread into cubes. Serve dip with bread and vegetables.

Makes 2½ cups

1 container (16 ounces) sour cream (2 cups)

1 box (10 ounces) frozen chopped spinach, thawed and squeezed dry

1 can (8 ounces) water chestnuts, rinsed, drained and chopped

1 packet (1 ounce) HIDDEN VALLEY® The Original Ranch® Salad Dressing & Seasoning Mix

1 loaf round French bread Fresh vegetables, for dipping

Louisiana Crab Dip with Crudités

1 package (8 ounces)
  cream cheese, softened
½ cup sour cream
3 tablespoons horseradish
2 tablespoons chopped
  fresh parsley
1 tablespoon coarse
  ground mustard
2 teaspoons TABASCO®
  brand Pepper Sauce
1 cup lump crabmeat
1 bunch baby carrots
1 bunch celery, cut into
  sticks
1 bunch asparagus spears,
  blanched
2 bunches endive
1 *each* red and green bell
  pepper, cored and cut
  into strips

Blend cream cheese, sour cream, horseradish, parsley, mustard and TABASCO® Sauce in medium bowl until well mixed. Stir in crabmeat.

Arrange carrots, celery, asparagus, endive and peppers on large platter. Serve with dip.   *Makes about 2 cups dip*

Dips & Dunks

Creamy Salsa Dip

In medium bowl, combine all ingredients except additional almonds and cilantro; mix well. Refrigerate at least 1 hour before serving. Garnish with additional almonds and cilantro. Serve with taco chips or fresh vegetables.

Makes about 2 cups

1½ cups prepared HIDDEN VALLEY® The Original Ranch® Dressing
2 tomatoes, peeled, seeded and chopped
½ cup shredded Monterey Jack cheese
¼ cup sliced almonds
¼ cup mild or hot green chile peppers,* seeded and minced
1 green onion, finely chopped
Additional sliced almonds
Fresh cilantro

Chile peppers can sting and irritate the skin. Wear rubber gloves when handling peppers and do not touch eyes.

Hot French Onion Dip

1 envelope LIPTON®
RECIPE SECRETS®
Onion Soup Mix
1 container (16 ounces)
sour cream
2 cups shredded Swiss
cheese (about
8 ounces)
¼ cup HELLMANN'S® or
BEST FOODS® Real
Mayonnaise

1. Preheat oven to 375°F. In 1-quart casserole, combine soup mix, sour cream, 1¾ cups Swiss cheese and mayonnaise.

2. Bake, uncovered, 20 minutes or until heated through. Sprinkle with remaining ¼ cup cheese.

3. Serve, if desired, with sliced French bread or your favorite dippers.

Makes 2 cups dip

Dips & Dunks

Spinach & Chèvre Dip

1. Place spinach, yogurt, cheese, mustard, basil, garlic and pepper in food processor or blender. Cover and process until well blended but slightly chunky. Cover and refrigerate 1 hour before serving.

2. Serve with vegetable crudités or crackers, if desired.

Makes 2 cups dip

Prep Time: *25 minutes*
Chill Time: *1 hour*

1 package (10 ounces) frozen chopped spinach, thawed and squeezed dry
1 cup plain nonfat yogurt
½ cup (2 ounces) crumbled goat cheese
¼ cup *French's®* Honey Dijon Mustard
2 tablespoons chopped fresh basil
1 clove garlic, chopped
¼ teaspoon black pepper

Zesty Cheese Fondue

1 package (1.8 ounces) white sauce mix
2 cups beer or nonalcoholic malt beverage
1 clove garlic, minced
1 package (16 ounces) pasteurized process cheese spread, cubed
3 tablespoons *Frank's® RedHot®* Original Cayenne Pepper Sauce
1 loaf French or Italian bread, cubed
Apple slices

1. Prepare white sauce mix in large saucepan according to package directions, substituting beer for milk and adding garlic. Stir in cheese; cook, stirring constantly, until cheese melts and sauce is smooth. Stir in *Frank's RedHot* Sauce.

2. Transfer sauce to fondue pot or heated chafing dish. Serve warm with bread cubes or apple slices.   *Makes 16 servings (4 cups)*

Prep Time: 15 minutes
Cook Time: 10 minutes

Dips & Dunks

Zesty Pesto Cheese Spread and Dip

1. Combine all ingredients in food processor. Cover and process until smooth and well blended.

2. Spoon pesto spread into serving bowl or crock. Spread on crackers or serve with vegetable crudités. *Makes 12 (¼-cup) servings*

Tip: To toast pine nuts, place nuts on baking sheet and bake at 350°F for 8 to 10 minutes or until lightly golden. Or, place nuts in microwavable dish and microwave on HIGH (100%) 1 minute.

Serving Suggestion: Use a pastry bag fitted with a decorative tip to pipe Pesto Spread into hollowed cherry tomatoes.

Prep Time: *15 minutes*

2 packages (8 ounces each) cream cheese, softened
1 cup shredded mozzarella cheese
1 cup chopped fresh basil or parsley
½ cup grated Parmesan cheese
½ cup pine nuts, toasted
⅓ cup *French's® Gourmayo™ Caesar Ranch*
1 teaspoon minced garlic

Sweets & Treats

Tart Cherry and Almond Sugar Plums

1 cup (about 6½ ounces)
   dried tart cherries
1 cup slivered almonds
5 teaspoons kirsch (cherry
   liqueur)
⅔ cup coarse white or
   colored sugar

1. Line medium baking dish with waxed paper; set aside.

2. Place cherries, almonds and kirsch in food processor; cover and process until mixture is finely chopped and comes together.

3. Place sugar in small bowl. Grease hands lightly. Shape fruit mixture into 1-inch balls. Roll balls, one at a time, in sugar to coat evenly. Place 1 inch apart in prepared baking dish. Let stand 20 to 30 minutes or until firm. Cover tightly and refrigerate up to 3 days. Serve candy pieces in decorative miniature baking cups, if desired. *Makes about 20 servings*

Quick Tiramisu

1 package (18 ounces) NESTLÉ® TOLL HOUSE® Refrigerated Sugar Cookie Bar Dough
1 package (8 ounces) ⅓-less-fat cream cheese
½ cup granulated sugar
¾ teaspoon TASTER'S CHOICE® 100% Pure Instant Coffee dissolved in ¾ cup cold water, *divided*
1 container (8 ounces) frozen nondairy whipped topping, thawed
1 tablespoon NESTLÉ® TOLL HOUSE® Baking Cocoa

PREHEAT oven to 325°F.

DIVIDE cookie dough into 20 pieces. Shape into 2½×1-inch oblong shapes. Place on ungreased baking sheets.

BAKE for 10 to 12 minutes or until light golden brown around edges. Cool on baking sheets for 1 minute; remove to wire racks to cool completely.

BEAT cream cheese and sugar in large mixer bowl until smooth. Beat in ¼ *cup* Taster's Choice. Fold in whipped topping. Layer 6 cookies in 8-inch-square baking dish. Sprinkle each cookie with *1 teaspoon* Taster's Choice. Spread *one-third* cream cheese mixture over cookies. Repeat layers 2 more times with *12* cookies, *remaining* coffee and *remaining* cream cheese mixture. Cover; refrigerate for 2 to 3 hours. Crumble *remaining* cookies over top. Sift cocoa over cookies. Cut into squares. *Makes 6 to 8 servings*

Brownie Cake Delight

1. Prepare brownies according to package directions in 11×7-inch baking pan. Cool completely in pan.

2. Whisk fruit spread in small bowl until smooth. Combine whipped topping and almond extract in medium bowl.

3. Cut brownie horizontally in half. Place half of brownie on serving dish. Spread with fruit spread and 1 cup whipped topping. Place second half of brownie, cut side down, over bottom layer. Spread with remaining whipped topping. Arrange strawberries on whipped topping. Drizzle chocolate syrup over cake before serving. Garnish with fresh mint, if desired.

Makes 16 servings

1 package (21 ounces) fudge brownie mix, plus ingredients to prepare mix
⅓ cup strawberry fruit spread
2 cups thawed frozen whipped topping
¼ teaspoon almond extract
2 cups strawberries, stemmed and halved
¼ cup chocolate syrup

Sweets & Treats

Grilled Banana Split

1 large firm ripe banana
½ teaspoon melted butter
2 tablespoons chocolate
  syrup
½ teaspoon orange liqueur
  (optional)
⅔ cup vanilla ice cream
2 tablespoons toasted
  sliced almonds

1. Prepare grill for direct cooking.

2. Cut unpeeled banana lengthwise in half; brush melted butter over cut sides. Grill halves, cut sides down, over medium-hot coals 2 minutes or until lightly browned; turn. Grill 2 minutes or until tender.

3. Combine syrup and liqueur, if desired, in small bowl. Cut banana halves in half crosswise; carefully remove peel. Place 2 pieces banana in each bowl; top with ⅓ cup ice cream, 1 tablespoon chocolate syrup and 1 tablespoon almonds. Serve immediately. *Makes 2 servings*

Sweets & Treats

Chocolate Truffle Cups

Heat crème fraîche over medium heat until it softens to a thick liquid consistency. Remove from heat and add chocolate. Stir until chocolate is melted and mixture is smooth. Add liqueur, if desired. Refrigerate for 1 hour or until set. Pipe into phyllo shells and serve.   *Makes 15 dessert cups*

1 (7-ounce) container ALOUETTE® Crème Fraîche
8 ounces good quality white or bittersweet chocolate, broken into small pieces
1 tablespoon liqueur, such as almond, coffee or orange (optional)
1 (2-ounce) package frozen mini phyllo shells

Refreshing Cocoa-Fruit Sherbet

1 medium ripe banana
1½ cups orange juice
1 cup (½ pint) half-and-half
½ cup sugar
¼ cup HERSHEY'S Cocoa

1. Slice banana into blender container. Add orange juice; cover and blend until smooth. Add remaining ingredients; cover and blend well. Pour into 8- or 9-inch square pan. Cover; freeze until hard around edges.

2. Spoon partially frozen mixture into blender container. Cover; blend until smooth but not melted. Pour into 1-quart mold. Cover; freeze until firm. Unmold onto cold plate and slice. Garnish as desired. *Makes 8 servings*

Variation: Add 2 teaspoons orange-flavored liqueur with orange juice.

Mango Coconut Tropical Freeze

1. Place mango, cream of coconut and lime juice in food processor; cover and process 1 to 2 minutes or until smooth.

2. Spoon mixture into 4 small dessert cups or custard cups. Top with pecans. Place cups on pie plate; cover tightly. Freeze 8 hours or overnight.

3. Remove from freezer and allow to thaw slightly before serving.

Makes 4 servings

1 jar (26 ounces) refrigerated mango slices, drained *or* 3 ripe mangoes, peeled and cut to equal about 3⅓ cups
½ cup canned cream of coconut
1 tablespoon lime juice
⅓ cup toasted chopped pecans

Bananas Foster

In 12-inch skillet, bring I Can't Believe It's Not Butter!® Spread, brown sugar and bananas to a boil. Cook 2 minutes, stirring gently. Carefully add rum to center of pan and cook 15 seconds. Serve hot banana mixture over scoops of ice cream and top, if desired, with sweetened whipped cream.

Makes 4 servings

Tip: Choose ripe but firm bananas for this recipe. They will hold their shape better when cooked.

Prep Time: *5 minutes*
Cook Time: *5 minutes*

6 tablespoons I CAN'T
BELIEVE IT'S NOT
BUTTER!® Spread
3 tablespoons firmly
packed brown sugar
4 medium ripe bananas,
sliced diagonally
2 tablespoons dark rum or
brandy (optional)
Vanilla ice cream

Peaches & Cream Gingersnap Cups

1. Combine gingersnap crumbs and ginger in small bowl; set aside.

2. Beat cream cheese in small bowl with electric mixer at medium speed until smooth. Add yogurt and vanilla. Beat at low speed until smooth and well blended. Stir in chopped peach.

3. Divide peach mixture between 2 (6-ounce) custard cups. Cover and refrigerate 1 hour. Top each serving with half of gingersnap crumb mixture just before serving. Garnish as desired. *Makes 2 servings*

Variation: Serve a whole gingersnap with each peach cup instead of crushing it to make the crumb mixture.

1½ tablespoons gingersnap
    crumbs (2 cookies)
¼ teaspoon ground ginger
2 ounces cream cheese,
    softened
1 container (6 ounces)
    peach yogurt
¼ teaspoon vanilla
⅓ cup chopped fresh peach
    or drained canned
    peach slices in juice

Easy Fruit Tarts

12 wonton skins
　　Vegetable cooking spray
2 tablespoons apple jelly or
　　apricot fruit spread
1½ cups sliced or cut-up
　　fruit such as DOLE®
　　Bananas, Strawberries
　　or Red or Green
　　Seedless Grapes
1 cup nonfat or low-fat
　　yogurt, any flavor

• Press wonton skins into 12 muffin cups sprayed with vegetable cooking spray, allowing corners to stand up over edges of muffin cups.

• Bake at 375°F 5 minutes or until lightly browned. Carefully remove wonton cups to wire rack; cool.

• Cook and stir jelly in small saucepan over low heat until jelly melts.

• Brush bottoms of cooled wonton cups with melted jelly. Place two fruit slices in each cup; spoon rounded tablespoon of yogurt on top of fruit. Garnish with fruit slice and mint leaf, if desired. Serve immediately.

Makes 12 servings

Prep Time: *20 minutes*
Bake Time: *5 minutes*

Punch Bowl Party Cake

1. Prepare cake mix and bake according to package directions for 13×9-inch cake; cool completely. Prepare pudding mix according to package directions.

2. Crumble half of cake into bottom of small punch bowl. Top with half of pudding.

3. Reserve a few cherries from cherry pie filling for garnish. Top pudding with half of cherry pie filling, nuts and whipped topping. Repeat layers, using remaining cake, pudding, cherry pie filling, nuts and whipped topping. Garnish with reserved cherries. *Makes 12 to 14 servings*

1 package (18¼ ounces) yellow cake mix, plus ingredients to prepare mix
1 package (4-serving size) instant vanilla pudding and pie filling mix, plus ingredients to prepare mix
2 containers (21 ounces each) cherry pie filling
1 cup chopped pecans
1 container (12 ounces) thawed frozen whipped topping

Rich Chocolate Mousse

1 cup (6 ounces) NESTLÉ®
  TOLL HOUSE® Semi-
  Sweet Chocolate
  Morsels
3 tablespoons butter, cut
  into pieces
2 teaspoons TASTER'S
  CHOICE® 100% Pure
  Instant Coffee
1 tablespoon hot water
2 teaspoons vanilla extract
½ cup heavy whipping
  cream

MICROWAVE morsels and butter in medium, uncovered, microwave-safe bowl on HIGH (100%) power for 1 minute. STIR. Morsels may retain some of their original shape. If necessary, microwave at additional 10- to 15-second intervals, stirring just until morsels are melted. Dissolve Taster's Choice in hot water; stir into chocolate. Stir in vanilla extract; cool to room temperature.

WHIP cream in small mixer bowl on high speed until stiff peaks form; fold into chocolate mixture. Spoon into tall glasses; refrigerate for 1 hour or until set. Garnish as desired.

Makes 2 servings

Poached Pears with Raspberry Sauce

Slow Cooker Directions

1. Combine juice, wine, sugar and cinnamon stick halves in slow cooker. Submerge pears in mixture. Cover; cook on LOW 3½ to 4 hours or until pears are tender. Remove and discard cinnamon sticks.

2. Process raspberries in food processor or blender until smooth; strain and discard seeds.

3. Spoon raspberry sauce onto serving plates; place pears on top of sauce. Garnish with fresh berries, if desired. *Makes 4 to 5 servings*

4 cups cran-raspberry juice cocktail
2 cups Rhine or Riesling wine
¼ cup sugar
2 cinnamon sticks, broken into halves
4 to 5 firm Bosc or Anjou pears, peeled*
1 package (10 ounces) frozen raspberries in syrup, thawed
Fresh berries for garnish (optional)

For a decorative touch, remove peel in spiral strips.

Chocolate Ice Cream Cups

2 cups (12 ounces) semi-sweet chocolate chips
1 (14-ounce) can EAGLE BRAND® Sweetened Condensed Milk (NOT evaporated milk)
1 cup finely ground pecans
Ice cream, any flavor

1. In heavy saucepan, over low heat, melt chocolate chips with EAGLE BRAND®; remove from heat. Stir in pecans. In individual paper-lined muffin cups, spread about 2 tablespoons chocolate mixture. With lightly greased spoon, spread chocolate on bottom and up side of each cup.

2. Freeze 2 hours or until firm. Before serving, remove paper liners. Fill chocolate cups with ice cream. Store unfilled cups tightly covered in freezer.

Makes about 1½ dozen cups

Note: The paper liners will be easier to remove if the chocolate cups sit at room temperature for about 5 minutes.

Sweets & Treats

Quick Berry Trifle

1. Combine berries and sugar in medium bowl, stirring gently to combine.

2. Place single layer of cake slices in bottom of deep serving bowl. Top with ⅓ of pudding, then ⅓ of berries. Repeat layers twice, using remaining ingredients. Cover tightly with plastic wrap and refrigerate at least 1 hour or until ready to serve.

3. Just before serving, top with dollop of whipped topping.

Makes 12 servings

2 cups fresh strawberry slices
1 cup fresh raspberries or blackberries
1 cup fresh blueberries
¼ cup sugar
1 pound cake (about 12 ounces), cut into ½-inch-thick slices
1 container (28 ounces) prepared vanilla pudding
1 can (7 ounces) aerosol whipped topping

Sweets & Treats

Chocolate Dream Torte

1 package DUNCAN
   HINES® Moist Deluxe®
   Dark Chocolate Fudge
   Cake Mix
1 (6-ounce) package
   semisweet chocolate
   chips, melted
1 (8-ounce) container
   frozen non-dairy
   whipped topping,
   thawed
1 container DUNCAN
   HINES® Creamy
   Home-Style Milk
   Chocolate Frosting
3 tablespoons finely
   chopped dry-roasted
   pistachios

1. Preheat oven to 350°F. Grease and flour two 9-inch round cake pans.

2. Prepare, bake and cool cake as directed on package for basic recipe.

3. For chocolate hearts garnish, spread melted chocolate to ⅛-inch thickness on waxed paper-lined baking sheet. Cut shapes with heart cookie cutter when chocolate begins to set. Refrigerate until firm. Push out heart shapes. Set aside.

4. To assemble, split each cake layer in half horizontally. Place one split cake layer on serving plate. Spread one-third of whipped topping on top. Repeat with remaining layers and whipped topping, ending with cake layer and leaving top plain. Frost side and top with frosting. Sprinkle pistachios on top. Position chocolate hearts by pushing points down into cake. Refrigerate until ready to serve. *Makes 12 to 16 servings*

Chocolate Strawberry Dream Torte: Omit semisweet chocolate chips and chopped pistachios. Proceed as directed through step 2. Fold 1½ cups chopped fresh strawberries into whipped topping in large bowl. Assemble as directed, filling torte with strawberry mixture and frosting with Milk Chocolate frosting. Garnish cake with strawberry fans and mint leaves, if desired.

Apple and Walnut Strudel

1. Thaw puff pastry according to package directions. Preheat oven to 375°F. Spray 2 baking sheets with nonstick cooking spray. Combine sour cream and egg yolk in small bowl; set aside. In separate small bowl, mix egg white and water; set aside.

2. On lightly floured surface, roll 1 pastry sheet into 12×10-inch rectangle. Spread ½ of apple pie filling down center ⅓ of pastry. Spread ½ cup sour cream mixture over filling; sprinkle with ½ cup walnuts.

3. Fold 1 long side of pastry over filling mixture; fold other side over filling mixture, overlapping edges. Press edges together to seal. Place on baking sheet, seam side down, tucking ends under. Using sharp knife, make 7 diagonal slits on top; brush with egg white mixture. Repeat steps 2 and 3 with remaining pastry, apple pie filling, sour cream mixture and walnuts. Bake 30 to 35 minutes or until golden brown. *Makes 16 servings*

1 package (about 17 ounces) frozen puff pastry
1 cup sour cream
1 egg, separated
1 tablespoon water
1 can (21 ounces) apple pie filling
1 cup coarsely chopped walnuts

Raspberry Almond Trifles

2 cups whipping cream
¼ cup plus 1 tablespoon raspberry liqueur or orange juice, divided
1 (14-ounce) can EAGLE BRAND® Sweetened Condensed Milk (NOT evaporated milk)
2 (3-ounce) packages ladyfingers, separated
1 cup seedless raspberry jam
½ cup sliced almonds, toasted

1. In large mixing bowl, beat whipping cream and 1 tablespoon liqueur until stiff peaks form. Fold in EAGLE BRAND®; set aside.

2. Layer bottom of 12 (4-ounce) custard cups or ramekins with ladyfingers. Brush with some remaining liqueur. Spread half of jam over ladyfingers. Spread evenly with half of cream mixture; sprinkle with half of almonds. Repeat layers with remaining ladyfingers, liqueur, jam, cream mixture and almonds. Cover and chill 2 hours. Store covered in refrigerator.

Makes 12 servings

Prep Time: *20 minutes*
Chill Time: *2 hours*

Speedy Pineapple-Lime Sorbet

1. Arrange pineapple in single layer on large baking sheet; freeze at least 1 hour or until very firm.*

2. Combine frozen pineapple, limeade, lime juice and lime peel in food processor; cover and process until smooth and fluffy. If mixture doesn't become smooth and fluffy, let stand 30 minutes to soften slightly; repeat processing.

3. Garnish as desired. Serve immediately.   *Makes 8 servings*

Pineapple can be frozen up to 1 month in resealable freezer food storage bags.

Note: This dessert is best if served immediately, but can be made ahead, stored in the freezer and then softened several minutes before being served.

1 ripe pineapple, cut into cubes (about 4 cups)
⅓ cup frozen limeade concentrate, thawed
1 to 2 tablespoons fresh lime juice
1 teaspoon grated lime peel

2 cups (11½-ounce package) HERSHEY'S Milk Chocolate Chips
½ cup light cream
½ teaspoon vanilla extract
Sweetened whipped cream (optional)

Milk Chocolate Pots de Crème

1. Place milk chocolate chips and light cream in medium microwave-safe bowl. Microwave on HIGH (100%) 1 minute or just until chips are melted and mixture is smooth when stirred. Stir in vanilla.

2. Pour into demitasse cups or very small dessert dishes. Cover; refrigerate until firm. Serve cold with sweetened whipped cream, if desired.

Makes 6 to 8 servings

Three-Melon Soup

1. Combine watermelon, pineapple juice and lemon juice in blender; cover and process until smooth. Chill at least 2 hours or overnight.

2. Scoop out balls of cantaloupe and honeydew.

3. To serve, pour watermelon mixture into shallow bowls; garnish with cantaloupe and honeydew.

Makes 4 servings

3 cups cubed seeded watermelon
3 tablespoons unsweetened pineapple juice
2 tablespoons lemon juice
¼ cantaloupe melon
⅛ honeydew melon

Raspberry Chantilly Parfait

1 container (8 ounces) vanilla yogurt

½ cup sifted powdered sugar

1 package (10 ounces) frozen raspberries in light syrup, thawed

4 cups thawed frozen whipped topping

1⅓ cups crushed oatmeal cookies or granola cereal

1⅓ cups fresh blueberries

1. Spread yogurt to ½-inch thickness on several layers of paper towels; place 2 layers of paper towels over yogurt. Let stand 15 minutes. Scrape yogurt from paper towels into large bowl. Stir in powdered sugar.

2. Place raspberries in food processor or blender; cover and process until smooth. Pour through fine-meshed sieve into bowl; press raspberries to squeeze out liquid. Discard seeds. Stir juice into yogurt. Fold in whipped topping.

3. Spoon ⅓ of yogurt mixture into 4 (8- to 12-ounce) stemmed glasses; sprinkle with half of crushed cookies and blueberries. Repeat layers, ending with yogurt mixture. Serve immediately, or cover and refrigerate up to 2 hours.

Makes 4 servings

Tip: To use whipped cream instead of whipped topping, beat 2 cups chilled whipping cream with ¼ cup powdered sugar until stiff peaks form. Fold into yogurt mixture and proceed as directed.

Sweets & Treats

Vanilla Ice Cream Loaf

1. Line 9×5-inch loaf pan with plastic wrap, leaving 2½-inch overhang on all sides. Combine powdered sugar and water in small bowl; stir until mixture resembles paste. Split ladyfingers. Spread small amount of powdered sugar mixture onto bottom of 1 ladyfinger and anchor it upright against side of pan. Repeat with remaining ladyfingers, making border around pan.

2. Beat ice cream in large bowl with electric mixer until smooth. Spread in pan, pressing against ladyfingers. Cover and freeze 6 hours.

3. Place loaf in refrigerator 20 minutes before serving. Using plastic overhang, carefully remove ice cream loaf from pan. To serve, drizzle 1 tablespoon sauce onto each serving plate. Cut loaf into slices; place over sauce. Drizzle additional 1 tablespoon sauce over each slice. Top with raspberries, if desired.

Makes 8 servings

¼ **cup powdered sugar**
1 to 2 teaspoons water
1 package (3 ounces) ladyfingers
1½ **quarts vanilla ice cream, softened**
Raspberry or strawberry sauce
Fresh or thawed frozen raspberries or strawberries (optional)

Cocoa Cappuccino Mousse

1 can (14 ounces) sweetened condensed milk (not evaporated milk)
⅓ cup HERSHEY'S Cocoa
3 tablespoons butter or margarine
2 teaspoons powdered instant coffee or espresso, dissolved in 2 teaspoons hot water
2 cups (1 pint) cold whipping cream

1. Combine sweetened condensed milk, cocoa, butter and coffee in medium saucepan. Cook over low heat, stirring constantly, until butter melts and mixture is smooth. Remove from heat; cool.

2. Beat whipping cream in large bowl until stiff. Gradually fold chocolate mixture into whipped cream. Spoon into dessert dishes. Refrigerate until set, about 2 hours. Garnish as desired.

Makes 8 servings

Prep Time: *15 minutes*
Cook Time: *10 minutes*
Chill Time: *2 hours*

Cheesecake-Filled Strawberries

1. Beat cream cheese 2 to 3 minutes in medium bowl with electric mixer at medium speed. Add powdered sugar and vanilla; beat until well blended.

2. Cut wedge out of side of each strawberry. Scoop out pulp, leaving ¼-inch shell; fill with cream cheese mixture. Top each strawberry with 2 toasted almonds.

3. Place strawberries on serving plate. Refrigerate until ready to serve.

Makes 4 to 6 servings

1 package (8 ounces) cream cheese, softened
1½ tablespoons powdered sugar
1½ teaspoons vanilla
1 pint whole fresh strawberries
1 package (8 ounces) sliced almonds, toasted

Wraps & Rolls

Grilled Chicken and Fresh Salsa Wraps

1¼ cups LAWRY'S® Herb & Garlic Marinade With Lemon Juice, divided

4 boneless, skinless chicken breasts (about 1 pound)

1 large tomato, chopped

1 can (4 ounces) diced green chiles, drained (optional)

¼ cup thinly sliced green onions

1 tablespoon red wine vinegar

1 tablespoon chopped fresh cilantro

½ teaspoon LAWRY'S® Garlic Salt

4 burrito-size *or* 8 fajita-size flour tortillas, warmed to soften

In large resealable plastic bag, combine 1 cup Herb & Garlic Marinade and chicken; seal bag and marinate in refrigerator at least 30 minutes. In medium bowl, combine tomato, chiles, onions, remaining ¼ cup Herb & Garlic Marinade, vinegar, cilantro and Garlic Salt; mix well. Cover and refrigerate 30 minutes or until chilled. Remove chicken from bag, discarding used marinade. Grill or broil chicken about 10 to 15 minutes, or until thoroughly cooked, turning halfway through grilling time. Slice chicken into strips. Place chicken on tortillas; spoon salsa mixture on top and wrap to enclose. Serve immediately.   *Makes 4 servings*

Meal Idea: This is an excellent recipe for picnics and outdoor dining. Wrap each filled tortilla with plastic wrap and keep chilled until ready to serve. You may also choose to assemble wraps when ready to serve outdoors!

Prep Time: 12 to 15 minutes
Marinate Time: 30 minutes
Cook Time: 10 to 15 minutes

Texas-Style Stuffed Pizza Bread

1 package (13.8 ounces) refrigerated pizza crust

1/3 cup *French's® Gourmayo*™ Smoked Chipotle Light Mayonnaise

1/2 pound sliced deli roast beef

1/4 pound sliced mozzarella or Jack cheese

1 jar (7 1/2 ounces) roasted red peppers, drained and sliced

1 cup sautéed onions*

1 teaspoon olive oil

1 teaspoon crushed oregano leaves

1 teaspoon minced garlic

To sauté onions, cook 1 1/2 cups sliced onions in 1 tablespoon oil for 5 minutes or until tender.

1. Heat oven to 425°F. Roll pizza dough into 13×10-inch rectangle on floured work surface. Spread mayonnaise evenly on dough. Layer roast beef and cheese on dough, overlapping slices, leaving a 1-inch border around edges. Top with peppers and onions.

2. Fold one third of dough toward center from long edge of rectangle. Fold second side toward center, enclosing filling. Tightly pinch long edge and ends to seal. Place seam-side down on greased baking sheet.

3. Brush with oil; sprinkle with oregano and garlic. Cut shallow slits crosswise along top of dough, spacing 3 inches apart. Bake 18 to 20 minutes or until deep golden brown. Remove to rack; cool slightly. Serve warm.

Makes 12 servings

Prep Time: *20 minutes*
Bake Time: *20 minutes*

Wraps & Rolls

Beefy Pinwheels

1. Place unwrapped cream cheese on paper plate. Microwave on HIGH 15 seconds or until softened. Combine cream cheese, olives and mustard in small bowl; mix well.

2. Spread about 2 tablespoons cream cheese mixture over each tortilla. Top each with 2 overlapping slices of beef.

3. Place onion on one edge of tortilla, trimming onion to fit diameter of tortilla. Roll up tortilla jelly-roll fashion. Cut each roll into slices to serve.

Makes 6 servings

1 package (8 ounces) cream cheese

¼ cup chopped pimiento-stuffed green olives

2 tablespoons prepared horseradish mustard

6 (6- to 7-inch) flour tortillas

12 small slices deli roast beef

6 green onions

Shrimp and Black Bean Wraps

4 large flour tortillas
1 tablespoon olive oil
8 ounces small shrimp, peeled and deveined
1 (15-ounce) can black beans, drained
1 large tomato, chopped
2 green onions, sliced
1½ teaspoons TABASCO® brand Pepper Sauce
½ teaspoon salt

Preheat oven to 375°F. Wrap tortillas in foil; place in oven 10 minutes to warm. Heat oil in 10-inch skillet over medium-high heat. Add shrimp; cook and stir until pink. Mash ½ cup beans in medium bowl; stir in remaining beans, shrimp, tomato, green onions, TABASCO® Sauce and salt. To assemble, place ¼ of mixture on each tortilla; roll up tortillas, tucking in sides.

Makes 4 servings

Wraps & Rolls

Cheddar Cheese and Rice Roll

PREP: CLEAN: Wash hands. Combine rice, Cheddar cheese, cream cheese, chilies and hot sauce. Mix by hand or in food processor. Shape mixture into a log. Roll in walnuts. Wrap tightly with plastic wrap and refrigerate 1 hour.

SERVE: Serve with assorted crackers.

CHILL: Refrigerate leftovers immediately.

Makes 15 servings

Prep Time: *20 minutes*
Cook Time: *none*

2 cups cooked UNCLE BEN'S® ORIGINAL CONVERTED® Brand Rice

3 cups grated low-fat Cheddar cheese

¾ cup fat-free cream cheese, softened

1 can (4½ ounces) green chilies, drained, chopped

⅛ teaspoon hot sauce

1½ cups chopped walnuts

Wraps & Rolls

Southwestern Quesadillas

3 (8-inch) flour tortillas
I CAN'T BELIEVE IT'S NOT BUTTER!® Spray
¼ teaspoon chili powder, divided
⅛ teaspoon ground cumin, divided
1 cup shredded Monterey Jack or Cheddar cheese (about 4 ounces)
1 can (4 ounces) chopped green chilies, drained
1 can (2¼ ounces) sliced pitted ripe olives, drained
2 tablespoons chopped cilantro (optional)

Generously spray one side of one tortilla with I Can't Believe It's Not Butter!® Spray. Sprinkle with ½ of the chili powder and cumin. On baking sheet, arrange tortilla spice-side down, then top with ½ of the cheese, chilies, olives and cilantro. Top with second tortilla. Repeat layers, ending with tortilla. Spray top tortilla generously with I Can't Believe It's Not Butter!® Spray, then sprinkle with remaining chili powder and cumin. Grill or broil until tortillas are golden and cheese is melted. Cut in wedges and serve, if desired, with salsa. *Makes 4 servings*

Honey Roasted Ham Biscuits

Heat oven to 400°F. Separate biscuits. Place in muffin pan cups, pressing gently into bottoms and up sides of cups. In bowl, combine ham, honey mustard and 2 tablespoons peanuts. Spoon ham mixture evenly into biscuit cups. Sprinkle with remaining 2 tablespoons peanuts. Bake 15 to 17 minutes.

Makes 10 servings

1 (10-ounce) can
    refrigerated buttermilk
    biscuits
2 cups (12 ounces) diced
    CURE 81® ham
½ cup honey mustard
¼ cup finely chopped
    honey-roasted peanuts,
    divided

Antipasto Crescent Bites

2 ounces cream cheese (do NOT use reduced-fat or fat-free cream cheese)

1 package (8 ounces) refrigerated crescent roll dough

1 egg plus 1 tablespoon water, beaten

4 (3×¾-inch) strips roasted red pepper

2 large marinated artichoke hearts, cut in half lengthwise

1 thin slice Genoa or other salami, cut into 4 strips

4 small stuffed green olives, cut into halves

1. Preheat oven to 375°F. Cut cream cheese into 16 equal pieces, about 1 teaspoon per piece; set aside. Remove dough from package. Unroll on lightly floured surface. Cut each dough triangle in half lengthwise to form 2 triangles. Brush edges of triangles lightly with egg mixture.

2. Wrap 1 red pepper strip around 1 piece of cream cheese. Place on dough triangle; fold over and pinch edges to seal. Place 1 piece of artichoke heart and 1 piece of cream cheese on dough triangle; fold over and pinch edges to seal. Wrap 1 salami strip around 1 piece of cream cheese. Place on dough triangle; fold over and pinch edges to seal. Place 2 olive halves and 1 piece of cream cheese on dough triangle; fold over and pinch edges to seal. Repeat with remaining red pepper strips, artichoke pieces, salami strips, olives, cream cheese and dough triangles. Place filled triangles evenly spaced on ungreased baking sheet. Brush with egg mixture.

3. Bake 12 to 14 minutes or until golden brown. Serve warm.

Makes 16 pieces

Crescent Rolls

Roasted Red Peppers

Artichoke Hearts MARINATED

Wraps & Rolls

Miniature Monte Cristos

Flatten each slice of trimmed bread with rolling pin. Spread slices with mustard. Top each with 1 slice each ham, turkey and Swiss cheese. Roll up bread tightly, using plastic wrap to assist in rolling. Wrap very tightly in plastic wrap to assure even log shape. Chill for 30 minutes.

For batter, in medium bowl beat together baking mix and eggs. Add evaporated milk, salt and cinnamon.

In deep-fat fryer or deep saucepan heat 1½ inches CRISCO® Oil to 375°F. Unwrap each roll and secure with 4 wooden picks. With serrated knife, slice each roll into 4 pieces (each secured with wooden pick).

Dip each piece in batter, allowing some batter to be absorbed. Fry a few pieces at a time in hot oil for 1 to 2 minutes or until deep golden brown, turning frequently. Drain on paper towels. Serve immediately or keep warm in 175°F oven. Serve with spicy mustard sauce, if desired.

Makes 2 dozen

Tip: To make a day ahead, prepare and fry as directed. Cool. Cover and refrigerate. Reheat in single layer on baking sheet in 425°F oven for 8 to 10 minutes.

6 slices soft white bread, crusts trimmed
Mustard
6 very thin slices fully cooked ham
6 very thin slices fully cooked turkey
6 very thin slices Swiss cheese
1 cup buttermilk baking mix
2 eggs
1 can (5⅓ ounces) evaporated milk
¼ teaspoon salt
⅛ teaspoon ground cinnamon
CRISCO® Oil for frying

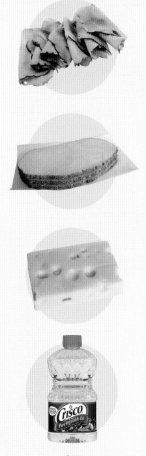

Rice & Artichoke Phyllo Triangles

1. Prepare rice according to package directions. Cool completely.

2. Preheat oven to 375°F. In medium bowl, combine rice, artichokes, Parmesan cheese and onion; mix well. Stir in yogurt until well blended.

3. Place one sheet of phyllo dough on a damp kitchen towel. (Keep remaining dough covered.) Lightly spray dough with nonstick cooking spray. Fold dough in half by bringing short sides together; spray lightly with additional cooking spray.

4. Cut dough into 4 equal strips, each about 3¼ inches wide. For each appetizer, spoon about 1 tablespoon rice mixture onto dough about 1 inch from end of each strip. Fold 1 corner over filling to make triangle. Continue folding, as you would fold a flag, to form a triangle that encloses filling. Repeat with remaining dough and filling.

5. Place triangles on greased baking sheets. Spray triangles with nonstick cooking spray. Bake 12 to 15 minutes or until golden brown.

Makes 40 appetizers

Cook's Tips: To simplify preparation, the rice mixture can be prepared a day ahead, covered and refrigerated until ready to use. Use a pizza cutter to cut phyllo dough into strips.

1 box UNCLE BEN'S®
   Butter & Herb Fast
   Cook Recipe Long
   Grain & Wild Rice
1 jar (6½ ounces)
   marinated quartered
   artichoke hearts,
   drained and finely
   chopped
2 tablespoons grated
   Parmesan cheese
1 tablespoon minced onion
   or 1 green onion with
   top, finely chopped
⅓ cup plain yogurt or sour
   cream
10 sheets frozen phyllo
   dough, thawed

Pastry Puffs with Goat Cheese and Spinach

Cook sausage in large skillet until browned. Drain on paper towels; let cool. Steam spinach; let cool. Preheat oven to 375°F. Cut 1 pastry sheet evenly into 9 squares. Cut 5 additional squares from second sheet (remaining pastry may be refrozen for future use). Stretch or roll squares slightly to form rectangles. Line each rectangle with 2 or 3 spinach leaves, leaving ¼ inch on 1 short end to seal edges. Spread about 1 teaspoon goat cheese over spinach; spread ½ teaspoon mustard over goat cheese. Arrange sausage across short end and roll up pastry and filling, pressing to seal edges. Place on *ungreased* baking sheet, seam sides down. Bake 14 to 16 minutes or until golden. Cut each puff into halves or thirds. Refrigerate leftovers.   *Makes 28 to 42 appetizers*

Note: Pastry puffs may be made ahead and refrigerated overnight or frozen up to 1 month. Reheat in oven when ready to serve.

1 (12-ounce) package BOB EVANS® Original Links
30 to 40 leaves fresh spinach
1 (17¾-ounce) package frozen puff pastry sheets, thawed according to package directions
⅓ cup goat cheese*
3 tablespoons Dijon mustard

*For a milder flavor, substitute plain or herb cream cheese for goat cheese.

Stuffed Party Baguette

2 medium red bell peppers
1 French bread loaf (about 14 inches long)
¼ cup plus 2 tablespoons Italian salad dressing, divided
1 small red onion, very thinly sliced
8 large fresh basil leaves
3 ounces Swiss cheese, very thinly sliced

1. Preheat oven to 425°F. Cover large baking sheet with foil; set aside. To roast bell peppers, cut peppers in half; remove stems, seeds and membranes. Place peppers, cut sides down, on prepared baking sheet. Bake 20 to 25 minutes or until skins are browned, turning occasionally. Transfer peppers from baking sheet to paper bag; close bag tightly. Let stand 10 minutes or until peppers are cool enough to handle and skins are loosened. Using sharp knife, peel off skins and discard. Cut peppers into strips.

2. Trim ends from bread; discard. Cut loaf lengthwise in half. Remove soft insides of loaf; reserve removed bread for another use, if desired. Brush ¼ cup Italian dressing evenly onto cut sides of bread. Arrange pepper strips in even layer in bottom half of loaf; top with even layer of onion. Brush onion with remaining 2 tablespoons Italian dressing; top with layer of basil and cheese. Replace bread top. Wrap loaf tightly in heavy-duty plastic wrap; refrigerate at least 2 hours or overnight.

3. When ready to serve, remove plastic wrap. Cut loaf crosswise into 1-inch slices. Secure with toothpicks and garnish, if desired.   *Makes 12 servings*

Buffalo-Style Wraps

1. Combine ⅓ *cup* **Frank's RedHot** Sauce and *1 tablespoon oil* in resealable plastic food storage bag. Add chicken. Seal bag; toss to coat evenly. Marinate in refrigerator 30 minutes or overnight.

2. Broil or grill chicken 10 to 15 minutes or until no longer pink in center. Slice chicken into long, thin strips. In bowl, toss chicken with remaining ⅓ *cup* **Frank's RedHot** Sauce and dressing.

3. Arrange chicken, lettuce and cheese down center of tortillas, dividing evenly. Fold bottom third of each tortilla over filling; fold sides towards center. Tightly roll up to secure filling. Cut in half to serve.

Makes 4 servings

Prep Time: *10 minutes*
Cook Time: *10 to 15 minutes*

⅔ cup *Frank's® RedHot®* **Original Cayenne Pepper Sauce, divided**
4 boneless skinless chicken breast halves
¼ cup **blue cheese salad dressing**
1 cup shredded lettuce
1 cup (4 ounces) shredded Monterey Jack cheese
4 (10-inch) flour tortillas, heated

Ham and Cheese Muffin Rolls

1 (1-pound) loaf frozen
    bread dough, thawed
3 tablespoons prepared
    mustard
1 tablespoon honey
2 cups shredded Swiss
    cheese
¾ pound very thinly sliced
    CURE 81® ham
   Mango chutney, if
    desired

On floured surface, roll dough into 21×12-inch rectangle. In small bowl, combine mustard and honey. Spread mustard mixture over dough. Sprinkle dough with cheese. Lay ham slices over cheese. Starting with long side, roll dough up tightly. Cut dough into 12 equal slices. Place slices, cut sides up, in greased muffin cups, pressing slightly. Cover. Let rise in warm place 45 minutes or until doubled in size. Heat oven to 375°F. Bake 30 minutes or until golden. Cover with foil if rolls become too brown. Serve with chutney, if desired.
Makes 12 appetizer servings

Pinwheel Ham Bites

1. Spread ½ package cheese to edges of each ham slice. Beginning at short end of ham slice, roll up tightly and wrap in plastic wrap. Refrigerate rolls at least 2 hours.

2. Cut each roll crosswise into 10 slices. Place 1 slice on each cracker. Serve immediately.   *Makes 40 appetizers*

2 packages (6½ ounces each) garlic-and-herb spreadable cheese, softened
4 (1/16-inch-thick) slices boiled ham
40 round buttery crackers

Chicken Parmesan Stromboli

1 pound boneless, skinless chicken breast halves
½ teaspoon salt
¼ teaspoon ground black pepper
2 teaspoons olive oil
2 cups shredded mozzarella cheese (about 8 ounces)
1 jar (1 pound 10 ounces) RAGÚ® Chunky Pasta Sauce, divided
2 tablespoons grated Parmesan cheese
1 tablespoon finely chopped fresh parsley
1 pound fresh or thawed frozen bread dough

1. Preheat oven to 400°F. Season chicken with salt and pepper. In 12-inch skillet, heat olive oil over medium-high heat and brown chicken. Remove chicken from skillet and let cool; pull into large shreds.

2. In medium bowl, combine chicken, mozzarella cheese, ½ cup Ragú Chunky Pasta Sauce, Parmesan cheese and parsley; set aside.

3. On greased jelly-roll pan, press dough to form 12×10-inch rectangle. Arrange chicken mixture down center of dough. Cover filling, bringing one long side into center, then overlap with the other long side; pinch seam to seal. Fold in ends and pinch to seal. Arrange on pan, seam-side down. Gently press in sides to form 12×4-inch loaf. Bake 35 minutes or until dough is cooked and golden. Cut stromboli into slices. Heat remaining pasta sauce and serve with stromboli.

Makes 6 servings

Mexican Roll-Ups

1. Cook lasagna noodles according to package directions, omitting salt. Rinse with cool water; drain. Cool.

2. Spread 2 tablespoons guacamole onto each noodle; top each with 2 tablespoons salsa and 2 tablespoons cheese.

3. Roll up noodles jelly-roll fashion. Cut each roll-up in half to form 2 equal-size roll-ups. Serve immediately with additional salsa, if desired, or cover with plastic wrap and refrigerate up to 3 hours.

Makes 12 servings

6 uncooked lasagna
   noodles
¾ cup prepared guacamole
¾ cup chunky salsa
¾ cup (3 ounces) shredded
   Cheddar cheese
Additional salsa
   (optional)

SPAM™ Pinwheels

1 (1-pound) loaf frozen
  bread dough, thawed
¼ cup pizza sauce
1 (7-ounce) can SPAM®
  Classic, cubed
2 cups (8 ounces) shredded
  mozzarella cheese
2 tablespoons chopped
  pepperoncini
  Additional pizza sauce

Roll bread dough out on lightly floured surface to 12-inch square. Brush pizza sauce over bread dough. Sprinkle SPAM®, cheese and pepperoncini over dough. Roll dough, jelly-roll fashion; pinch seam to seal (do not seal ends). Cut roll into 16 slices. Place slices, cut side down, on greased baking sheet. Cover and let rise in warm place 45 minutes. Heat oven to 350°F. Bake 20 to 25 minutes or until golden brown. Serve immediately with additional pizza sauce.

Makes 16 appetizer servings

Jamaican Jerk Turkey Wraps

1. Prepare grill for direct cooking. Rub jerk seasoning on both sides of turkey.

2. Grill turkey over medium coals 15 to 20 minutes or until turkey is no longer pink in center and juices run clear, turning once. Thinly slice turkey.

3. Place broccoli slaw, tomato, dressing, jalapeño peppers and mustard, if desired, in large bowl; toss gently to mix. Place sliced turkey on tortillas; spoon broccoli slaw mixture on top. Wrap to enclose. Serve immediately.

Makes 4 servings

1½ teaspoons Caribbean jerk seasoning
6 ounces turkey breast tenderloin
4 cups broccoli slaw
1 large tomato, seeded and chopped (about 1⅓ cups)
⅓ cup coleslaw dressing
2 jalapeño peppers,* finely chopped
2 tablespoons prepared mustard (optional)
8 (8-inch) flour tortillas, warmed

Jalapeño peppers can sting and irritate the skin. Wear rubber gloves when handling peppers and do not touch eyes. Wash hands after handling.

Veggie Quesadilla Appetizers

10 (8-inch) flour tortillas
1 cup finely chopped broccoli
1 cup thinly sliced small mushrooms
¾ cup shredded carrots
¼ cup chopped green onions
1¼ cups (5 ounces) sharp Cheddar cheese
2 cups salsa

1. Brush both sides of tortillas lightly with water. Heat small nonstick skillet over medium heat until hot. Heat tortillas, one at a time, 30 seconds on each side. Divide vegetables among 5 tortillas; sprinkle evenly with cheese. Top with remaining 5 tortillas.

2. Cook quesadillas, one at a time, in large nonstick skillet or on griddle over medium heat 2 minutes on each side or until surface is crisp and cheese is melted.

3. Cut each quesadilla into 4 wedges. Serve with salsa.

Makes 20 servings

Little Turkey Travelers

Combine mild peppers, artichoke hearts, giardiniera and roasted peppers in medium bowl. Spread cream cheese on each flat bread. Place turkey and cheese slices on each bread; top each with 1½ cups vegetable mixture.* Roll tightly, jelly-roll style, beginning at the filled end. Wrap each roll in plastic wrap. Chill 2 hours. Cut each roll into 16 slices.   *Makes 48 appetizers*

For better roll sealing, leave 4 inches across top of each bread covered with cream cheese only.

Preparation Time: *30 minutes plus chilling time*

2 pounds BUTTERBALL®
   Peppered Turkey
   Breast, sliced thin in
   the deli
1 jar (16 ounces) mild
   pepper rings, drained
1 can (14 ounces)
   artichoke hearts,
   drained and quartered
1 jar (8 ounces) mild
   giardiniera, undrained
1 jar (7 ounces) roasted red
   peppers, drained and
   cut into wide strips
2 packages (8 ounces each)
   soft cream cheese with
   chives and onion
1 package (17 ounces) soft
   cracker bread (three
   16-inch round flat
   breads)
½ pound thinly sliced
   provolone cheese

Sausage Pinwheels

2 cups biscuit mix
½ cup milk
¼ cup butter or margarine, melted
1 pound BOB EVANS® Original Recipe Roll Sausage

Combine biscuit mix, milk and butter in large bowl until blended. Refrigerate 30 minutes. Divide dough into two portions. Roll out one portion on floured surface to ⅛-inch-thick rectangle, about 10×7 inches. Spread with half the sausage. Roll lengthwise into long roll. Repeat with remaining dough and sausage. Place rolls in freezer until firm enough to cut easily. Preheat oven to 400°F. Cut rolls into thin slices. Place on baking sheets. Bake 15 minutes or until golden brown. Serve hot. Refrigerate leftovers. *Makes 48 pinwheels*

Note: This recipe may be doubled. Refreeze after slicing. When ready to serve, thaw slices in refrigerator and bake.

Muffaletta Wraps

1. In a small bowl, combine olives, pickled vegetables, parsley and olive oil; mix well. (Olive mixture may be covered and refrigerated up to 1 day before serving.)

2. For each wrap, line a tortilla with a lettuce leaf, 2 ounces salami and 2 slices cheese. Top with a heaping ¼ cup olive mixture. Fold ends in and roll up tortilla. Wrap in plastic wrap and refrigerate until serving time. (May be prepared up to 4 hours before serving.) *Makes 4 servings*

Preparation Time: *20 minutes*

½ cup chopped pimiento-stuffed olives
½ cup chopped pitted kalamata or ripe olives
½ cup chopped drained bottled hot pickled vegetables
¼ cup chopped parsley
2 tablespoons olive oil
4 large (10-inch) flour tortillas or flavored tortillas
4 large leaves red leaf lettuce
½ pound sliced Genoa or hard salami
8 slices SARGENTO® Deli Style Sliced Provolone Cheese

Make-Ahead Southwestern Chili Cheese Empanadas

3/4 cup (3 ounces) finely shredded taco-flavored cheese*

1/3 cup diced green chilies, drained

1 package (15 ounces) refrigerated pie crusts

1 egg

Chili powder

*If taco-flavored cheese is unavailable, toss 3/4 cup shredded Colby Jack cheese with 1/2 teaspoon chili powder.

1. Combine cheese and chilies in small bowl. Unfold 1 pastry crust on floured surface. Roll into 13-inch circle. Cut dough into 16 rounds using 3-inch cookie cutter, rerolling scraps as necessary. Repeat with remaining crust to make 32 circles. Spoon 1 teaspoon cheese mixture in center of each dough round. Fold round in half, sealing edge with tines of fork.

2. Place empanadas on wax paper-lined baking sheets; freeze, uncovered, 1 hour or until firm. Place in resealable food storage bags. Freeze up to 2 months, if desired.

3. To complete recipe, preheat oven to 400°F. Place frozen empanadas on ungreased baking sheet. Beat egg and 1 tablespoon water in small bowl; brush on empanadas. Sprinkle with chili powder. Bake 12 to 17 minutes or until golden brown. Remove from baking sheet to wire rack to cool.

Makes 32 servings

Serving Suggestion: Serve empanadas with salsa and sour cream.

Chicken Roll-Ups

1. Preheat oven to 400°F. Spray baking dish with nonstick cooking spray. Spread 1 cup marinara sauce in bottom of dish.

2. Pound chicken breasts between 2 sheets of plastic wrap to about ¼-inch thickness with flat side of meat mallet or rolling pin. Press ½ cup spinach leaves onto each chicken breast. Top each with 1 slice mozzarella. Roll up tightly.

3. Place each chicken roll, seam side down, in baking dish. Cover with remaining marinara. Cover with foil. Bake 35 minutes. Remove foil. Continue baking 10 minutes. Garnish with Parmesan cheese and red pepper flakes, if desired.   *Makes 4 servings*

2½ cups marinara sauce, divided
4 boneless skinless chicken breasts (about ¼ pound each)
2 cups fresh baby spinach leaves
4 slices (1 ounce each) mozzarella cheese
4 tablespoons grated Parmesan cheese
Red pepper flakes (optional)

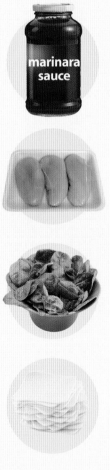

Ham and Cheese "Sushi" Rolls

4 thin slices deli ham (about 4×4 inches)

1 package (8 ounces) cream cheese, softened

1 piece (4 inches long) seedless cucumber, quartered lengthwise (about ½ cucumber)

4 thin slices (about 4×4 inches) American or Cheddar cheese, at room temperature

1 red bell pepper, cut into thin 4-inch-long strips

1. For ham sushi, pat 1 ham slice with paper towel to remove excess moisture. Spread 2 tablespoons cream cheese to edges of ham slice. Pat 1 cucumber piece with paper towel to remove excess moisture; place at edge of ham slice. Roll up tightly, pressing gently to seal. Wrap in plastic wrap; refrigerate. Repeat with remaining ham slices, cream cheese and cucumber pieces to make 4 rolls.

2. For cheese sushi, spread 2 tablespoons cream cheese to edges of 1 cheese slice. Place 2 strips red pepper at edge of cheese slice. Roll up tightly, pressing gently to seal. Wrap in plastic wrap; refrigerate. Repeat with remaining cheese slices, cream cheese and red pepper strips to make 4 rolls.

3. To serve, remove plastic wrap from ham and cheese rolls. Cut each roll into 8 (½-inch-thick) pieces. *Makes 8 (8-piece) servings*

Sweet Potato Phyllo Wraps

1. Preheat oven to 375°F. Line baking sheet with parchment paper. Mash sweet potatoes with vanilla and ground cinnamon.

2. Unroll phyllo dough in a stack of 4 sheets. Cover with waxed paper and damp kitchen towel. Remove 1 sheet; spray edges lightly and evenly with cooking spray. Spread 3 tablespoons sweet potato mixture along 1 short edge of phyllo. Sprinkle with 1 tablespoon chopped pecans. Quickly roll up. Slice into thirds and place on prepared baking sheet. Repeat with remaining phyllo sheets.

3. Spray tops of phyllo wraps with cooking spray. Bake 15 to 20 minutes or until golden brown. Drizzle with maple syrup. Garnish with strawberries, if desired. *Makes 4 servings*

¾ **cup mashed sweet potatoes**
¾ **teaspoon vanilla**
½ **teaspoon ground cinnamon**
4 **(16½×12-inch) sheets frozen phyllo dough, thawed**
  Butter-flavored nonstick cooking spray
4 **tablespoons finely chopped pecans**
1 **tablespoon light maple syrup**
  Fresh strawberries (optional)

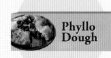

Wraps & Rolls

Grill & Chill

Marinated Flank Steak with Pineapple

1 can (15¼ ounces) DEL MONTE® Sliced Pineapple In Its Own Juice
¼ cup teriyaki sauce
2 tablespoons honey
1 pound beef flank steak

1. Drain pineapple, reserving 2 tablespoons juice. Set aside pineapple for later use.

2. Combine reserved juice, teriyaki sauce and honey in shallow 2-quart dish; mix well. Add meat; turn to coat. Cover and refrigerate at least 30 minutes or overnight.

3. Remove meat from marinade, reserving marinade. Grill meat over hot coals (or broil), brushing occasionally with reserved marinade. Cook about 4 minutes on each side for rare; about 5 minutes on each side for medium; or about 6 minutes on each side for well done. During last 4 minutes of cooking, grill pineapple until heated through.

4. Slice meat across grain; serve with pineapple. Garnish, if desired.

Makes 4 servings

Note: Do not baste meat during last 5 minutes of cooking. Marinade that has come into contact with raw meat must be discarded or boiled for several minutes before being served with cooked food.

Prep and Marinate Time: *35 minutes*
Cook Time: *10 minutes*

Rosemary-Crusted Leg of Lamb

¼ cup Dijon mustard
2 large cloves garlic, minced
1 boneless butterflied leg of lamb (sirloin half, about 2½ pounds), well trimmed
3 tablespoons chopped fresh rosemary *or* 1 tablespoon dried rosemary
Fresh rosemary sprigs (optional)
Mint jelly (optional)

1. Prepare grill for direct cooking.

2. Combine mustard and garlic in small bowl; spread half of mixture over one side of lamb. Sprinkle with half of chopped rosemary; pat into mustard mixture. Turn lamb over; repeat with remaining mustard mixture and rosemary. Insert meat thermometer into center of thickest part of lamb. Place lamb on grid. Grill, covered, over medium coals 35 to 40 minutes or until thermometer registers 160°F for medium or until desired doneness is reached, turning every 10 minutes.

3. Meanwhile, soak rosemary sprigs in water, if desired. Place rosemary sprigs directly on coals during last 10 minutes of grilling. Transfer lamb to carving board; tent with foil. Let stand 10 minutes before carving into thin slices. Serve with mint jelly, if desired. *Makes 8 servings*

Chocolate-Caramel S'Mores

1. Prepare coals for grilling.

2. Place 6 wafer cookies top-down on plate. Spread 1 teaspoon caramel topping in center of each wafer to within about ¼ inch of edge.

3. Spear 1 to 2 marshmallows onto long, wood-handled skewer.* Hold several inches above coals 3 to 5 minutes or until marshmallows are golden and very soft, turning slowly. Push 1 marshmallow off into center of caramel. Top with remaining plain wafer cookie. Repeat with remaining wafers, topping and marshmallows. *Makes 6 servings*

*If wood-handled skewers are unavailable, use oven mitt to protect hand from heat.

Tip: S'Mores, a favorite campfire treat, got their name because everyone who tasted them wanted "some more." In the unlikely event of leftover S'Mores, they can be reheated in the microwave on HIGH 5 to 10 seconds.

12 chocolate wafer cookies or chocolate graham cracker squares
2 tablespoons fat-free caramel ice cream topping
6 large marshmallows

Turkey-Ham Quesadillas

¼ cup picante sauce or salsa
4 (7-inch) flour tortillas
½ cup shredded Monterey Jack cheese
¼ cup finely chopped turkey-ham or lean ham
¼ cup canned diced green chilies, drained
Nonstick cooking spray
Additional picante sauce or salsa for dipping (optional)
Sour cream (optional)

1. Spread 1 tablespoon picante sauce on each tortilla.

2. Sprinkle cheese, turkey ham and chilies equally over half of each tortilla. Fold over uncovered half to make quesadilla. Spray tops and bottoms of quesadillas with cooking spray.

3. Grill on uncovered grill over medium coals 1½ minutes per side or until cheese is melted and tortillas are golden brown, turning once. Quarter each quesadilla and serve with additional picante sauce and sour cream, if desired.

Makes 8 servings

Grill & Chill

Grilled Honey Garlic Pork Chops

Combine all ingredients except pork chops in small bowl. Place pork in shallow baking dish; pour marinade over pork. Cover and refrigerate 4 hours or overnight. Remove pork from marinade. Heat remaining marinade in small saucepan over medium heat to a simmer. Grill pork over medium-hot coals 12 to 15 minutes, turning once during cooking and basting frequently with marinade, until meat thermometer registers 155° to 160°F.

Makes 4 servings

Favorite recipe from **National Honey Board**

¼ **cup lemon juice**
¼ **cup honey**
 2 **tablespoons soy sauce**
 1 **tablespoon dry sherry**
 2 **cloves garlic, minced**
 4 **boneless center-cut lean pork chops (about 4 ounces each)**

Grilled Coriander Corn

4 ears fresh corn
3 tablespoons butter or margarine, softened
1 teaspoon ground coriander
¼ teaspoon salt
⅛ teaspoon ground red pepper

1. Pull outer husks from top to base of each corn; leave husks attached to ear. (If desired, remove 1 strip of husk from inner portion of each ear; reserve for later use.) Strip away silk from corn. Place corn in large bowl. Cover with cold water; soak 20 to 30 minutes.

2. Meanwhile, prepare grill for direct cooking. Remove corn from water; pat kernels dry with paper towels. Combine butter, coriander, salt and ground red pepper in small bowl. Spread evenly with spatula over kernels.

3. Bring husks back up each ear of corn; secure at top with paper-covered metal twist-ties. (Or, use reserved strips of corn husk to tie knots at the top of each ear, if desired.) Place corn on grid. Grill corn on covered grill over medium-hot coals 20 to 25 minutes or until corn is hot and tender, turning halfway through grilling time with tongs. *Makes 4 servings*

Note: For ember cooking, prepare corn as recipe directs, but omit soaking in cold water. Wrap each ear securely in heavy-duty foil. Place directly on coals. Grill corn on covered grill over medium-hot coals 25 to 30 minutes or until corn is hot and tender, turning every 10 minutes with tongs.

Grilled Portobello Mushroom Sandwiches

1. Brush mushrooms, bell pepper, onion slices and cut sides of buns with some dressing; set buns aside. Grill vegetables over medium-hot coals 2 minutes.

2. Turn vegetables over; brush with dressing. Grill 2 minutes more or until vegetables are tender. Remove bell pepper and onion slices from grill.

3. Place bun halves, cut sides down, on grill. Turn mushrooms, top side up; brush with any remaining dressing and cover with cheese, if desired. Grill 1 minute or until cheese is melted and buns are lightly toasted. Cut pepper into strips. Place mushrooms on bottom halves of buns; top with onion slices and pepper strips. Cover with top halves of buns.   *Makes 2 servings*

Note: To broil, brush mushrooms, bell pepper, onion slices and cut sides of buns with dressing. Place vegetables on greased rack of broiler pan; set buns aside. Broil vegetables 4 to 6 inches from heat 3 minutes; turn over. Brush with dressing. Broil 3 minutes more or until vegetables are tender. Place mushrooms, top side up, on broiler pan; cover with cheese, if desired. Place buns, cut sides up, on broiler pan. Broil 1 minute or until cheese is melted and buns are toasted. Assemble sandwiches as directed above.

2 large portobello
   mushrooms, cleaned
   and stemmed
½ medium green bell
   pepper, cut into
   quarters
2 thin slices red onion
2 whole wheat hamburger
   buns, split
¼ cup Italian salad dressing
2 slices (1 ounce each)
   mozzarella cheese
   (optional)

Rosemary's Chicken

4 large boneless skinless chicken breast halves (about 1½ pounds)
¼ cup *French's*® Classic Yellow® Mustard
¼ cup frozen orange juice concentrate, undiluted
2 tablespoons cider vinegar
2 teaspoons dried rosemary leaves, crushed
4 strips thick sliced bacon

Place chicken in large resealable plastic food storage bag or glass bowl. To prepare marinade, combine mustard, orange juice concentrate, vinegar and rosemary in small bowl. Pour over chicken. Seal bag or cover bowl and marinate in refrigerator 30 minutes. Wrap 1 strip bacon around each piece of chicken; secure with toothpicks.*

Place chicken on grid, reserving marinade. Grill over medium coals 25 minutes or until chicken is no longer pink in center, turning and basting often with marinade. (Do not baste during last 10 minutes of cooking.) Remove toothpicks before serving. Garnish as desired.   *Makes 4 servings*

Soak toothpicks in water 20 minutes to prevent burning.

Prep Time: *15 minutes*
Marinate Time: *30 minutes*
Cook Time: *25 minutes*

Skewered Beef Strips with Spicy Honey Glaze

1. Slice beef across the grain into ¼-inch-thick strips. Thread beef strips onto 12 wooden skewers* and place in large glass baking dish.

2. Prepare grill for direct cooking. Combine soy sauce, vinegar, ginger and red pepper; pour over skewers and marinate 10 minutes, turning once. Drain marinade into small saucepan; stir in honey and brush mixture over beef. Bring remaining mixture to a boil; boil 2 minutes.

3. Grill skewered beef 3 to 4 minutes. Serve remaining honey glaze as dipping sauce.   *Makes 4 servings*

Soak skewers in cold water 20 minutes before using to prevent them from burning.

Serving Suggestion: Try these scrumptious skewers over a bed of rice or Chinese egg noodles.

1 beef top sirloin steak
   (about 1 pound)
⅓ cup soy sauce
2 tablespoons white
   vinegar
1 teaspoon ground ginger
⅛ teaspoon ground red
   pepper
⅓ cup honey

Texas Barbecued Ribs

1 cup GRANDMA'S®
    Molasses
½ cup coarse-grained
    mustard
2 tablespoons cider vinegar
2 teaspoons dry mustard
3½ pounds pork loin baby
    back ribs or spareribs,
    cut into 6 sections

Prepare grill for direct cooking. In medium bowl, combine molasses, mustard, cider vinegar and dry mustard. When ready to cook, place ribs on grill, meaty side up, over medium-hot coals. Grill 1 to 1¼ hours or until meat is tender and starts to pull away from bone, basting frequently with sauce* during last 15 minutes of grilling. To serve, carefully cut ribs apart with knife and arrange on platter.   *Makes 4 servings*

*Do not baste during last 5 minutes of grilling.

Fresco Marinated Chicken

1. For marinade, blend all ingredients except chicken.

2. In shallow baking dish or plastic bag, pour ½ cup of the marinade over chicken. Cover, or close bag, and marinate in refrigerator, turning occasionally, up to 3 hours. Refrigerate remaining marinade.

3. Remove chicken, discarding marinade. Grill or broil chicken, turning once and brushing with refrigerated marinade until chicken is thoroughly cooked.

Makes 4 servings

1 envelope **LIPTON®**
    RECIPE SECRETS®
    Savory Herb with
    Garlic Soup Mix*
⅓ **cup water**
¼ **cup BERTOLLI® Olive Oil**
1 **teaspoon lemon juice or**
    vinegar
4 **boneless, skinless**
    chicken breast halves
    (about 1¼ pounds)

*Also terrific with LIPTON® RECIPE SECRETS® Golden Onion Soup Mix.

Sizzling Florida Shrimp

1½ pounds Florida Shrimp, peeled and deveined
1 cup Florida mushrooms, cut into halves
½ cup Florida red bell pepper pieces (1-inch pieces)
½ cup Florida onion pieces (1-inch pieces)
1 (8.9-ounce) jar lemon pepper sauce *or* 1 cup barbecue sauce

Arrange shrimp on wooden skewers with mushrooms, red bell pepper and onion. Place skewers in glass dish and cover with sauce, reserving about 2 tablespoons for basting during cooking. Cover and refrigerate for 1 hour. Prepare grill surface by cleaning and coating with oil. Coals are ready when coals are no longer flaming but are covered with gray ash. Place skewers on grill about 6 inches from coals. Grill shrimp for about 3 to 4 minutes on each side, basting with reserved sauce before turning once. Serve with sautéed asparagus and grilled garlic bread.   *Makes 4 servings*

Favorite recipe from **Florida Department of Agriculture and Consumer Services, Bureau of Seafood and Aquaculture**

Southwest Steak

1. Place dressing, parsley, *Frank's RedHot* Sauce, lime juice and Worcestershire in blender or food processor. Cover; process until smooth. Reserve ⅔ cup sauce. Pour remaining sauce over steak in deep dish. Cover; refrigerate 30 minutes.

2. Grill or broil steak 8 minutes per side for medium-rare or to desired doneness. Let stand 5 minutes. Slice steak and serve with reserved ⅔ cup sauce.

Makes 6 to 8 servings

Prep Time: *10 minutes*
Marinate Time: *30 minutes*
Cook Time: *20 minutes*

¾ cup Italian dressing
½ cup minced fresh parsley
⅓ cup *Frank's® RedHot®* Original Cayenne Pepper Sauce
3 tablespoons lime juice
1 tablespoon *French's®* Worcestershire Sauce
2 pounds boneless sirloin or top round steak (1½ inches thick)

Grilled Oriental Shrimp Kabobs

3 tablespoons soy sauce
1 tablespoon regular or seasoned rice vinegar
1 tablespoon dark sesame oil
2 cloves garlic, minced
¼ teaspoon red pepper flakes
1 pound large raw shrimp, peeled and deveined

1. For marinade, combine soy sauce, vinegar, oil, garlic and red pepper flakes in small bowl; mix well. Cover; refrigerate up to 3 days.

2. Combine marinade and shrimp in large resealable food storage bag. Seal bag securely. Refrigerate at least 30 minutes or up to 2 hours, turning bag once.

3. Spray grid with nonstick cooking spray. Prepare grill for direct cooking. Drain shrimp, reserving marinade. Thread shrimp onto 4 (12-inch) skewers. Place skewers on prepared grid; brush with half of reserved marinade. Grill skewers on covered grill over medium coals 5 minutes. Turn skewers over; brush with remaining marinade. Grill 3 to 5 minutes more or until shrimp are opaque. *Makes 4 servings*

Serving Suggestion: Serve with fried rice and fresh pineapple spears, if desired.

All-American Onion Burger

Combine beef, Worcestershire, ⅔ *cup* French Fried Onions, garlic salt and pepper. Form into 4 patties. Place patties on grid. Grill over hot coals about 10 minutes or until meat thermometer inserted into beef reaches 160°F, turning once. Top with remaining ⅔ *cup* onions. Serve on rolls.

Makes 4 servings

Luscious Oniony Cheeseburger: Place 1 slice cheese on each burger before topping with French Fried Onions.

Tangy Western Burger: Top each burger with 1 tablespoon barbecue sauce and 1 strip crisp bacon before topping with French Fried Onions.

California Burger: Combine 2 tablespoons *each* mayonnaise, sour cream and *French's®* Bold n' Spicy Brown Mustard in small bowl; spoon over burgers. Top each burger with avocado slices, sprouts and French Fried Onions.

Salisbury Steak Burger: Prepare 1 package brown gravy mix according to directions. Stir in 1 can (4 ounces) drained sliced mushrooms. Spoon over burgers and top with French Fried Onions.

Pizza Burger: Top each burger with pizza sauce, mozzarella cheese and French Fried Onions.

Chili Burger: Combine 1 can (15 ounces) chili without beans, 2 tablespoons *Frank's RedHot* Sauce and 2 teaspoons *each* chili powder and ground cumin. Cook until heated through. Spoon over burgers and top with French Fried Onions.

Prep Time: *10 minutes*
Cook Time: *10 minutes*

1 pound ground beef
2 tablespoons *French's®* Worcestershire Sauce
1⅓ cups *French's®* French Fried Onions, divided
½ teaspoon garlic salt
¼ teaspoon ground black pepper
4 hamburger rolls

Grilled Sherry Pork Chops

¼ cup **HOLLAND HOUSE®**
  Sherry Cooking Wine
¼ cup **GRANDMA'S®**
  Molasses
2 tablespoons soy sauce
4 pork chops (1 inch thick)

In plastic bowl, combine sherry, molasses and soy sauce; pour over pork chops. Cover; refrigerate 30 minutes. Prepare grill. Drain pork chops; reserve marinade. Grill pork chops over medium-high heat 20 to 30 minutes or until pork is no longer pink in center, turning once and brushing frequently with reserved marinade.* Discard any remaining marinade. *Makes 4 servings*

Do not baste during last 5 minutes of grilling.

Herbed Beef Kabobs

In large resealable plastic bag, combine ¾ cup Herb & Garlic Marinade and beef. Seal bag and marinate in refrigerator for 30 minutes, turning several times. Remove beef from bag, discarding used marinade. Onto skewers, alternate beef with vegetables until all are used. Grill or broil to desired degree of doneness, about 10 to 14 minutes, brushing with remaining ¼ cup Marinade.

Makes 4 to 6 servings

Meal Idea: Serve with your favorite rice dish or baked potatoes.

Hint: Soak wooden skewers in water for at least 15 minutes before using to help reduce burning.

Prep Time: 15 minutes
Marinate Time: 30 minutes
Cook Time: 10 to 14 minutes

1 cup LAWRY'S® Herb & Garlic Marinade With Lemon Juice, divided
1 to 1½ pounds boneless beef top sirloin, cut into chunks
12 mushrooms
2 medium green bell peppers, cut into 1½-inch squares
2 medium onions, cut into chunks
Skewers

Grill & Chill

Peppercorn Steaks

2 tablespoons olive oil
1 to 2 teaspoons cracked
    pink or black
    peppercorns
    or black pepper
1 teaspoon minced garlic
1 teaspoon dried herbs,
    such as rosemary or
    parsley
4 boneless beef top loin
    (strip) or ribeye steaks
    (6 ounces each)
¼ teaspoon salt

1. Combine oil, peppercorns, garlic and herbs in small bowl. Rub mixture onto both sides of each steak. Cover and refrigerate.

2. Prepare grill for direct cooking.

3. Place steaks on grid over medium heat. Grill, uncovered, 10 to 12 minutes for medium-rare to medium, or to desired doneness, turning occasionally. Season with salt after cooking.

Makes 4 servings

BBQ Corn Wheels

1. Cut corn into ½-inch slices. Alternately thread corn and pepper chunks onto four metal skewers. (Pierce tip of skewer through center of corn wheel to thread.) Combine barbecue sauce, honey and Worcestershire.

2. Coat kabobs with vegetable cooking spray. Grill kabobs on greased rack over medium heat for 5 minutes. Cook 5 minutes more until corn is tender, turning and basting with barbecue sauce mixture. Serve any extra sauce on the side with grilled hamburgers, steaks or chicken.   *Makes 4 servings*

Prep Time: *10 minutes*
Cook Time: *10 minutes*

4 ears corn on the cob, husked and cleaned
3 red, green or yellow bell peppers, cut into large chunks
¾ cup barbecue sauce
½ cup honey
¼ cup *French's*® Worcestershire Sauce
Vegetable cooking spray

½ cup Dijon mustard
1 tablespoon red wine vinegar
1 teaspoon ground red pepper
4 red snapper fillets (about 6 ounces each)
Fresh parsley sprigs and red peppercorns (optional)

Mustard-Grilled Red Snapper

1. Spray grid with nonstick cooking spray. Prepare grill for direct cooking.

2. Combine mustard, vinegar and pepper in small bowl; mix well. Coat fish thoroughly with mustard mixture.

3. Place fish on grid. Grill, covered, over medium-high heat 8 minutes or until fish flakes easily when tested with fork, turning halfway through grilling time. Garnish with parsley sprigs and red peppercorns, if desired.

Makes 4 servings

Orange Mustard Ham Kabobs

In small bowl, combine barbecue sauce and marmalade; mix well. Remove ½ cup mixture for basting; reserve remaining mixture. Thread ham and orange wedges on skewers. Brush with ½ cup barbecue sauce mixture reserved for basting. Grill over medium-hot coals 10 minutes or until browned, turning frequently and basting with remaining barbecue mixture. Serve with reserved sauce mixture.   *Makes 6 servings*

Alternate Method: Orange Mustard Ham Kabobs can also be broiled 6 inches from heat source 10 minutes or until browned.

¾ cup honey mustard
   barbecue sauce
½ cup orange marmalade
1½ pounds CURE 81® ham,
   cut into 1-inch cubes
2 small oranges, cut into
   6 wedges each

Grilled Salmon Fillets, Asparagus and Onions

½ teaspoon paprika
6 salmon fillets (6 to 8 ounces each)
⅓ cup bottled barbecue sauce or honey-Dijon marinade
1 bunch (about 1 pound) fresh asparagus spears, ends trimmed
1 large red or sweet onion, cut into ¼-inch-thick slices
1 tablespoon olive oil
Salt and black pepper

1. Prepare grill for direct cooking. Sprinkle paprika over salmon fillets. Brush barbecue sauce over salmon; let stand at room temperature 15 minutes.

2. Brush asparagus and onion slices with olive oil; season to taste with salt and pepper.

3. Place salmon, skin side down, in center of grid over medium coals. Arrange asparagus spears and onion slices around salmon. Grill salmon and vegetables on covered grill 5 minutes. Turn salmon, asparagus and onion slices. Grill 5 to 6 minutes more or until salmon flakes when tested with a fork and vegetables are crisp-tender. Separate onion slices into rings; arrange over asparagus.

Makes 6 servings

Grilled Sausage Kabobs with Apricot Mustard Sauce

1. Prepare grill for direct cooking. Combine preserves and mustard in small bowl; mix well.

2. Thread sausage, apricots and mushrooms onto 4 skewers. Brush with ¼ of preserve mixture.

3. Grill over medium-hot coals 8 minutes, turning once. Baste with ½ of remaining preserve mixture. Continue grilling 2 minutes more, turning once, or until sausage is lightly browned. Serve kabobs with remaining ¼ of preserve mixture for dipping.   *Makes 4 servings*

Note: Andouille sausage is a spicy, smoked pork sausage often used in Cajun and Creole cooking.

¾ cup apricot preserves
¾ cup Dijon mustard
1 pound smoked andouille or other pork sausage, cut into 1½-inch pieces
16 dried apricot halves
16 medium whole mushrooms

Spiced Turkey with Fruit Salsa

6 ounces turkey breast
   tenderloin
2 teaspoons lime juice
1 teaspoon mesquite
   seasoning blend or
   ground cumin
½ cup frozen pitted sweet
   cherries, thawed* and
   cut into halves
¼ cup chunky salsa

*Drained canned sweet cherries can
be substituted for frozen cherries.*

1. Prepare grill for direct cooking. Brush both sides of turkey with lime juice. Sprinkle with mesquite seasoning.

2. Grill turkey over medium coals 15 to 20 minutes or until turkey is no longer pink in center and juices run clear, turning once.

3. Meanwhile, stir together cherries and salsa. Thinly slice turkey. Spoon salsa mixture over turkey.

Makes 2 servings

Dark Sweet Cherries

SALSA

Grill & Chill

Grilled Garlic-Pepper Shrimp

1. Prepare grill for direct cooking.

2. Meanwhile, combine oil, lemon juice and garlic-pepper in large resealable food storage bag; add shrimp. Marinate 20 to 30 minutes in refrigerator, turning bag once.

3. Thread 5 shrimp onto each of 4 skewers; discard marinade. Grill on grid over medium heat 6 minutes or until shrimp are pink and opaque. Serve with lemon wedges, if desired. *Makes 4 servings*

⅓ cup olive oil
2 tablespoons lemon juice
1 teaspoon garlic-pepper blend
20 jumbo raw shrimp, peeled and deveined
Lemon wedges (optional)

Kids & Fun

Ice Cream Cone Cakes

1 package (about 18 ounces) devil's food cake mix, plus ingredients to prepare mix

$\frac{1}{3}$ cup sour cream

18 flat-bottomed ice cream cones

$4\frac{1}{2}$ cups ice cream (any flavor)

Cake decorations or chocolate sprinkles

1. Preheat oven to 350°F. Grease and flour 8- or 9-inch round cake pan; set aside.

2. Prepare cake mix according to package directions, substituting sour cream for $\frac{1}{3}$ cup of the water and decreasing oil to $\frac{1}{4}$ cup. Spoon $\frac{1}{2}$ of batter (about $2\frac{1}{3}$ cups) evenly into ice cream cones, using about 2 tablespoons batter for each. Pour remaining batter into prepared cake pan.

3. Stand cones on baking sheet. Bake cones and cake layer until toothpick inserted into centers comes out clean, about 20 minutes for cones and about 35 minutes for cake layer. Cool cones completely on wire racks. Cool cake layer 10 minutes. Remove to wire rack; cool completely. Reserve or freeze cake layer for another use. Top each filled cone with $\frac{1}{4}$ cup scoop of ice cream just before serving. Sprinkle with decorations as desired. Serve immediately.

Makes 18 cone cakes

1 package (18 ounces)
   refrigerated sugar or
   peanut butter cookie
   dough
All-purpose flour
   (optional)
1 cup (6 ounces) semisweet
   chocolate chips
1 tablespoon plus
   2 teaspoons
   shortening, divided
¼ cup white chocolate
   chips
Gummy fruit, chocolate-
   covered peanuts,
   assorted roasted nuts,
   raisins, jelly beans and
   other assorted candies
   for toppings

Cookie Pizza

1. Preheat oven to 350°F. Generously grease 12-inch pizza pan. Remove dough from wrapper. Sprinkle dough with flour to minimize sticking, if necessary. Press dough into bottom of prepared pan, leaving about ¾ inch between edge of dough and edge of pan. Bake 14 to 23 minutes or until golden brown and set in center. Cool completely in pan on wire rack, running spatula between cookie and pan after 10 to 15 minutes to loosen.

2. Melt semisweet chocolate chips and 1 tablespoon shortening in microwavable bowl on HIGH 1 minute; stir. Repeat process at 10- to 20-second intervals until smooth. Melt white chocolate chips and remaining 2 teaspoons shortening in another microwavable bowl on MEDIUM-HIGH (70%) 1 minute; stir. Repeat process at 10- to 20-second intervals until smooth.

3. Spread melted semisweet chocolate mixture over crust to within 1 inch of edge. Decorate with desired toppings. Drizzle melted white chocolate over toppings to resemble melted mozzarella cheese. Cut and serve.

Makes 10 to 12 pizza slices

Ultimate Rocky Road Cups

Preheat oven to 350°F. Generously grease 24 (2½-inch) muffin cups or line with foil liners. Place butter and chocolate in large microwave-safe bowl. Microwave on HIGH 1 minute; stir. Microwave on HIGH an additional 30 seconds; stir until chocolate is completely melted. Add sugar and eggs, one at a time, beating well after each addition; blend in flour. In separate bowl combine "M&M's"® Chocolate Mini Baking Bits and nuts; stir 1 cup baking bits mixture into brownie batter. Divide batter evenly among prepared muffin cups. Bake 20 minutes. Combine remaining baking bits mixture with marshmallows; divide evenly among muffin cups, topping hot brownies. Return to oven; bake 5 minutes longer. Cool completely before removing from muffin cups. Store in tightly covered container.   *Makes 24 cups*

Mini Ultimate Rocky Road Cups: Prepare recipe as directed, dividing batter among 60 generously greased 2-inch mini muffin cups. Bake 15 minutes. Sprinkle with topping mixture; bake 5 minutes longer. Cool completely before removing from cups. Store in tightly covered container. Makes about 60 mini cups.

Ultimate Rocky Road Squares: Prepare recipe as directed, spreading batter into generously greased 13×9×2-inch baking pan. Bake 30 minutes. Sprinkle with topping mixture; bake 5 minutes longer. Cool completely. Cut into squares. Store in tightly covered container. Makes 24 squares.

¾ cup (1½ sticks) butter or margarine
4 squares (1 ounce each) unsweetened baking chocolate
1½ cups granulated sugar
3 large eggs
1 cup all-purpose flour
1¾ cups "M&M's"® Chocolate Mini Baking Bits
¾ cup coarsely chopped peanuts
1 cup mini marshmallows

Banana Smoothies & Pops

1 (14-ounce) can EAGLE
    BRAND® Sweetened
    Condensed Milk (NOT
    evaporated milk)
1 (8-ounce) container
    vanilla yogurt
2 ripe bananas
½ cup orange juice

1. In blender container, combine all ingredients; blend until smooth. Stop occasionally to scrape down sides.

2. Serve immediately. Store leftovers covered in refrigerator.

Makes 4 cups

Banana Smoothie Pops: Spoon banana mixture into 8 (5-ounce) paper cups. Freeze 30 minutes. Insert wooden craft sticks into the center of each cup; freeze until firm. Makes 8 pops.

Fruit Smoothies: Substitute 1 cup of your favorite fruit and ½ cup any fruit juice for banana and orange juice.

Prep Time: *5 minutes*

S'Mores Snack Cake

1. Preheat oven to 350°F. Grease 13×9-inch baking pan.

2. Prepare cake mix according to package directions. Spread batter in prepared pan. Sprinkle with ½ cup chocolate chunks. Bake 30 minutes.

3. Remove cake from oven; sprinkle with remaining ½ cup chocolate chunks and marshmallows. Arrange bears evenly over top of cake. Return cake to oven; bake 8 minutes or until marshmallows are golden brown. Cool completely before cutting.   *Makes 24 servings*

Note: This cake is best served the day it is made.

1 package (18¼ ounces) yellow cake mix with pudding in the mix, plus ingredients to prepare mix
1 cup chocolate chunks, divided
1½ cups miniature marshmallows
1 cup bear-shaped graham crackers (honey or chocolate flavor)

Kids & Fun

Dizzy Dogs

1 package refrigerated
    breadstick dough
    (8 breadsticks)
1 package (16 ounces) hot
    dogs (8 hot dogs)
1 egg white
    Sesame seeds and poppy
    seeds
    Mustard, ketchup and
    barbecue sauce
    (optional)

1. Preheat oven to 375°F.

2. Using 1 piece breadstick dough for each, wrap hot dogs with dough in spiral pattern. Brush breadstick dough with egg white and sprinkle with sesame seeds and poppy seeds. Place on ungreased baking sheet.

3. Bake 12 to 15 minutes or until light golden brown. Serve with condiments for dipping, if desired.

Makes 8 servings

Kids & Fun

Chocolate Peanut Butter Candy Bars

1. Preheat oven to 350°F. Lightly grease 13×9-inch baking pan.

2. Combine cake mix, evaporated milk and butter in large bowl; beat with electric mixer at medium speed until well blended. (Dough will be stiff.) Spread ⅔ of dough in prepared pan. Sprinkle with peanuts.

3. Bake 10 minutes; remove from oven and sprinkle with chopped candy. Drop remaining dough by large spoonfuls over candy. Bake 15 to 20 minutes or until set. Cool completely on wire rack.   *Makes 24 servings*

1 package (18¼ ounces) devil's food or dark chocolate cake mix *without* pudding in the mix
1 can (5 ounces) evaporated milk
⅓ cup butter, melted
½ cup dry-roasted peanuts
4 packages (1½ ounces each) chocolate peanut butter cups, coarsely chopped

Cinnamon Apple Chips

2 cups unsweetened apple juice
1 cinnamon stick
2 Washington Red Delicious apples

1. In large skillet or saucepan, combine apple juice and cinnamon stick; bring to a low boil while preparing apples.

2. With paring knife, slice off ½ inch from tops and bottoms of apples and discard (or eat). Stand apples on either cut end; cut crosswise into ⅛-inch-thick slices, rotating apple, as necessary, to cut even slices.

3. Drop slices into boiling juice; cook 4 to 5 minutes or until slices appear translucent and lightly golden. Meanwhile, preheat oven to 250°F.

4. With slotted spatula, remove apple slices from juice and pat dry. Arrange slices on wire racks, making sure none overlap. Place racks on middle shelf in oven; bake 30 to 40 minutes until slices are lightly browned and almost dry to the touch. Let chips cool on racks completely before storing in airtight container. *Makes about 40 chips*

Tip: There is no need to core apples because boiling in juice for several minutes softens core and removes seeds.

Favorite recipe from **Washington Apple Commission**

Ice Cream Sandwiches

1. Preheat oven to 350°F. Lightly spray 13×9-inch pan with nonstick cooking spray. Line pan with aluminum foil and spray again.

2. Beat cake mix, eggs, water and melted butter in large bowl with electric mixer at medium speed until well blended. (Dough will be thick and sticky.) Spoon dough into prepared pan. Cover with plastic wrap and press dough evenly into pan, using plastic wrap to keep hands from sticking to dough. Remove plastic wrap and prick surface all over with fork (about 40 times) to prevent dough from rising too much.

3. Bake 20 minutes or until toothpick inserted into center comes out clean. Cool completely in pan on wire rack. Cut cookie in half crosswise; remove one half from pan. Spread ice cream evenly over cookie half remaining in pan. Top with second half; use foil in pan to wrap up sandwich. Freeze at least 4 hours. Cut into 8 equal pieces; dip cut ends in sugar or sprinkles. Wrap sandwiches individually and freeze until ready to serve.

Makes 8 sandwiches

Peppermint Ice Cream Sandwiches: Stir ⅓ cup crushed peppermint candies into vanilla ice cream before assembling. Roll ends of sandwiches in additional crushed peppermint candies to coat.

Tip: If the ice cream is too hard to scoop easily, microwave on HIGH 10 seconds to soften.

1 package (18¼ ounces) chocolate cake mix with pudding in the mix
2 eggs
¼ cup warm water
3 tablespoons butter or margarine, melted
1 pint vanilla ice cream, softened
Colored decorating sugar or sprinkles

Chicken Nuggets with Barbecue Dipping Sauce

1 pound boneless skinless chicken breasts
¼ cup all-purpose flour
¼ teaspoon salt
Dash black pepper
2 cups crushed baked cheese crackers
1 teaspoon dried oregano
1 egg white
1 tablespoon water
3 tablespoons barbecue sauce
2 tablespoons peach or apricot fruit spread

1. Preheat oven to 400°F. Cut chicken into 40 (1-inch) pieces. Place flour, salt and pepper in large resealable food storage bag. Combine cracker crumbs and oregano in shallow bowl. Whisk together egg white and water in small bowl.

2. Place 6 to 8 chicken pieces in bag with flour mixture; seal bag. Shake until chicken is coated. Remove chicken from bag; shake off excess flour. Coat all sides of chicken pieces with egg white mixture. Roll in crumb mixture. Place in shallow baking pan. Repeat with remaining chicken pieces. Bake 10 to 13 minutes or until golden brown.

3. Meanwhile, combine barbecue sauce and jam in small saucepan. Cook and stir over low heat until heated through. Serve chicken nuggets with dipping sauce.
Makes 8 servings

Note: To freeze chicken nuggets, cool 5 minutes on baking sheet. Wrap chicken in plastic wrap, making packages of 5 nuggets each. Place packages in freezer container or plastic freezer bag. Freeze. To reheat nuggets, preheat oven to 325°F. Unwrap nuggets. Place nuggets on ungreased baking sheet. Bake for 13 to 15 minutes or until hot. Or, place 4 to 5 nuggets on microwavable plate. Microwave on DEFROST (30%) 2½ to 3½ minutes or until hot, turning once. For each serving, stir together about 1½ teaspoons barbecue sauce and ½ teaspoon jam in small microwavable dish. Microwave on HIGH 10 to 15 seconds or until hot.

Twisty Sticks

1. Remove dough from wrapper. Divide dough in half; place in separate medium bowls. Let dough stand at room temperature about 15 minutes. Add 3 tablespoons flour and cocoa powder to one dough half; beat at medium speed of electric mixer until well blended. Add remaining 3 tablespoons flour and peanut butter to other dough half; beat at medium speed of electric mixer until well blended. Wrap halves separately in plastic wrap; refrigerate at least 1 hour.

2. Preheat oven to 350°F. Divide chocolate dough into 30 equal pieces. Divide peanut butter dough into 30 equal pieces. Shape each dough piece into 4-inch-long rope on lightly floured surface. For each cookie, twist 1 chocolate rope and 1 peanut butter rope together. Place 2 inches apart on ungreased cookie sheets. Bake 7 to 10 minutes or until set. Remove to wire rack; cool completely.

3. Meanwhile, combine chocolate chips and shortening in small microwavable bowl. Microwave on HIGH 1 minute; stir. Microwave on HIGH for additional 30-second intervals until chips and shortening are completely melted and smooth. Spread chocolate on 1 end of each cookie; top with sprinkles and peanuts as desired. Place on waxed paper. Let stand 30 minutes or until set.

Makes 2½ dozen cookies

1 package (18 ounces) refrigerated sugar cookie dough
6 tablespoons all-purpose flour, divided
1 tablespoon unsweetened cocoa powder
2 tablespoons creamy peanut butter
1 cup semisweet chocolate chips
1 tablespoon shortening
Colored sprinkles and finely chopped peanuts

Kids & Fun

Peanut Butter and Chocolate Spirals

1 package (18 ounces) refrigerated sugar cookie dough
1 package (18 ounces) refrigerated peanut butter cookie dough
¼ cup unsweetened cocoa powder
⅓ cup peanut butter chips, chopped
¼ cup all-purpose flour
⅓ cup miniature chocolate chips

1. Remove doughs from wrappers. Combine sugar cookie dough and cocoa in large bowl. Stir in peanut butter chips. Place peanut butter cookie dough and flour in another large bowl. Stir in chocolate chips. Divide each dough in half; cover and refrigerate 1 hour.

2. Roll each dough on floured surface to 12×6-inch rectangle. Layer each half of peanut butter dough onto each half of chocolate dough. Roll up doughs, starting at long end to form 2 (12-inch) rolls. Wrap in plastic wrap; refrigerate 1 hour.

3. Preheat oven to 375°F. Cut dough into ½-inch-thick slices. Place cookies 2 inches apart on ungreased cookie sheets. Bake 10 to 12 minutes or until lightly browned. Remove to wire racks; cool completely.

Makes 4 dozen cookies

Kids & Fun

Sandwich Cookies

1. Preheat oven to 350°F. Grease cookie sheets. Remove dough from wrapper. Divide dough into 4 equal sections. Reserve 1 section; refrigerate remaining 3 sections.

2. Roll reserved dough to ¼-inch thickness. Sprinkle with flour to minimize sticking, if necessary. Cut out cookies using ¾-inch round or fluted cookie cutter. Transfer cookies to prepared cookie sheets, placing about 2 inches apart. Repeat with remaining dough.

3. Bake 8 to 11 minutes or until edges are lightly browned. Remove to wire racks; cool completely. To make sandwich, spread about 1 tablespoon desired filling on flat side of 1 cookie to within ¼ inch of edge. Top with second cookie, pressing gently. Roll side of sandwich in desired decorations. Repeat with remaining cookies.   *Makes about 20 to 24 sandwich cookies*

Tip: Be creative—make sandwich cookies using 2 or more flavors of refrigerated cookie dough. Mix and match to see how many flavor combinations you can come up with.

1 package (18 ounces) refrigerated cookie dough, any flavor
All-purpose flour as needed
Any combination of colored frostings, peanut butter or assorted ice creams for filling
Colored sprinkles, chocolate-covered raisins, miniature candy-coated chocolate pieces and other assorted small candies for decoration

Cheeseburger Macaroni

1. Cook pasta according to package directions; drain.

2. Brown meat with onion in large skillet; drain. Season with salt and pepper, if desired. Stir in undrained tomatoes, ketchup and pasta; heat through.

3. Top with cheese. Garnish, if desired.

Makes 4 servings

Prep Time: *8 minutes*
Cook Time: *15 minutes*

1 cup mostaccioli or elbow macaroni, uncooked
1 pound ground beef
1 medium onion, chopped
1 can (14½ ounces) DEL MONTE® Diced Tomatoes with Basil, Garlic & Oregano
¼ cup DEL MONTE® Tomato Ketchup
1 cup (4 ounces) shredded Cheddar cheese

Kids & Fun

Brownie Gems

1. Preheat oven to 350°F. Spray (1¾-inch) mini-muffin pans with vegetable cooking spray or line with foil baking cups.

2. Combine brownie mix, fudge packet from mix, eggs, water and oil in large bowl. Stir with spoon until well blended, about 50 strokes. Drop 1 heaping teaspoonful of batter into each muffin cup; top with candy. Cover candy with more batter. Bake at 350°F for 15 to 17 minutes.

3. Cool 5 minutes. Carefully loosen brownies from pan. Remove to wire racks to cool completely. Frost and decorate as desired.

Makes 30 brownie gems

1 package DUNCAN HINES® Chocolate Lover's® Double Fudge Brownie Mix
2 eggs
2 tablespoons water
⅓ cup vegetable oil
28 miniature peanut butter cup or chocolate kiss candies
1 container of your favorite Duncan Hines frosting

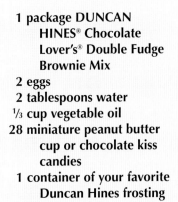

Kids & Fun

Rocky Road Sandwiches

1 package (18 ounces) refrigerated chocolate chip cookie dough

¼ cup unsweetened cocoa powder

1 cup marshmallow creme

6 ounces (⅔ cup) cream cheese, softened

1 cup finely chopped nuts

1. Preheat oven to 350°F. Grease cookie sheets. Remove dough from wrapper; place in large bowl. Let dough stand at room temperature about 15 minutes.

2. Add cocoa to dough in bowl; beat at medium speed of electric mixer until well blended. Drop dough by rounded teaspoonfuls onto prepared cookie sheets. Bake 8 to 10 minutes or until set and no longer shiny. Remove to wire rack; cool completely.

3. For filling, combine marshmallow creme and cream cheese in medium bowl; beat at medium speed of electric mixer until well blended. Place 1 tablespoon filling on flat side of cookie. Top with second cookie; press down to allow filling to squeeze out slightly between cookies. Roll filled edge in chopped nuts. Repeat with remaining cookies, filling and nuts.

Makes about 1½ dozen sandwich cookies

Kids & Fun

Rainbow Cake

1. Prepare cake mix and bake in 2 (8-inch) round cake pans according to package directions. Cool in pans on wire racks 15 minutes. Remove from pans to wire racks; cool completely.

2. Place 1 layer upside down on serving platter. Spread raspberry jam on top. Add second cake layer upside down to make flat cake top. Frost entire cake with vanilla frosting.

3. Place string in straight line across center of cake; lift string to remove. Using line left by string as guide, position row of red candies across cake and down side. Place row of orange candies on both sides of red row across top and down side. Repeat with remaining candies in order of colors of the rainbow: yellow, green, violet. Add row of candies around base of cake, alternating colors.   *Makes 12 servings*

Variation: This exceptionally easy cake leaves lots of room for personal creativity. Instead of a rainbow, position the candies in spokes like a color wheel or in diagonal stripes spaced an inch or two apart. Or simply sprinkle the top of the cake with candies for a festive polka dot look.

1 package (18 ounces) cake mix (any flavor), plus ingredients to prepare mix
⅓ cup raspberry jam
1 container (16 ounces) vanilla frosting
Multi-colored coated fruit candies (at least 5 different colors)

Frozen Florida Monkey Malt

2 bananas, peeled
5 tablespoons frozen
  orange juice
  concentrate
1 cup milk
3 tablespoons malted milk
  powder (optional)

1. Wrap bananas in plastic wrap; freeze.

2. Break bananas into pieces; place in blender with orange juice concentrate, milk and malted milk powder, if desired; blend until smooth.

3. Pour into fun glasses to serve.

Makes 2 servings

Kids & Fun

Funny Face Pizzas

1. Heat oven to 425°F. Spray baking sheet with nonstick cooking spray; set aside.

2. Remove dough from package. *Do not unroll dough.* Slice dough into 4 equal pieces. Knead each piece of dough until ball forms. Pat or roll each ball into 4-inch disk. Place disks on prepared baking sheet.

3. Spread ¼ cup sauce onto each disk. Sprinkle with mozzarella cheese. Decorate with toppings to create faces. Sprinkle with Cheddar cheese to resemble hair. Bake 10 minutes or until cheese is just melted and bottoms of pizzas are light brown.

Makes 4 servings

1 package (10 ounces) refrigerated pizza dough
1 cup pizza sauce
1 cup (4 ounces) shredded mozzarella cheese
Assorted toppings: pepperoni, black olive slices, green or red bell pepper slices, mushroom slices
⅓ cup shredded Cheddar cheese

Pupcakes

1 package (18¼ ounces) chocolate cake mix, plus ingredients to prepare mix
½ cup (1 stick) butter, softened
4 cups powdered sugar
¼ to ½ cup half-and-half or milk
Red and yellow fruit roll-ups
Assorted colored jelly beans and candy-coated chocolate pieces

1. Preheat oven to 350°F. Line 24 standard (2½-inch) muffin pan cups with paper liners. Prepare cake mix and bake in prepared pans according to package directions. Cool cupcakes in pans on wire racks 15 minutes; remove from pans and cool completely on wire racks.

2. Beat butter in large bowl with electric mixer at medium speed until creamy. Gradually add powdered sugar to form very stiff frosting, scraping down side of bowl occasionally. Gradually add half-and-half until frosting is of desired consistency.

3. Generously frost tops of cupcakes. Cut out ear and tongue shapes from fruit roll-ups with scissors; arrange on cupcakes, pressing into frosting as shown in photo. Add candies to create eyes and noses.

Makes 24 cupcakes

Rainbow Pastel Parfaits

1. Prepare pudding mixes according to package directions. Spread decorating sugars on 3 small, separate plates. Wet rims of 8 parfait glasses with damp paper towel. Invert glasses onto plates of sugar and coat rims of glasses with varying colors of sugar. Set glasses upright on tray to dry.

2. Stir strawberry gelatin powder into vanilla pudding, one teaspoon at a time, until desired shade of pink is reached. Fill each glass about ⅓ full with vanilla pudding mixture. Add layer of lemon pudding and layer of pistachio pudding.

3. Top each parfait with a dollop of whipped topping and any remaining sugar sprinkles, if desired.

Makes 8 servings

1 package (4-serving size) instant vanilla-flavored pudding mix
1 package (4-serving size) instant lemon-flavored pudding mix
1 package (4-serving size) instant pistachio-flavored pudding mix
2 tablespoons *each* pink, green and yellow decorating sugars
1 tablespoon strawberry gelatin powder (from 4-serving size box)
½ cup thawed frozen whipped topping

Kids & Fun

Acknowledgments

The publisher would like to thank the companies and organizations listed below for the use of their recipes and photographs in this publication.

Alouette® Cheese, Chavrie® Cheese, Saladena®

Bob Evans®

Butterball® Turkey

Crisco is a registered trademark of The J.M. Smucker Company

Del Monte Corporation

Dole Food Company, Inc.

Duncan Hines® and Moist Deluxe® are registered trademarks of Pinnacle Foods Corp.

Eagle Brand®

Florida Department of Agriculture and Consumer Services, Bureau of Seafood and Aquaculture

Grandma's® is a registered trademark of Mott's, LLP

The Hershey Company

The Hidden Valley® Food Products Company

Hillshire Farm®

Holland House® is a registered trademark of Mott's, LLP

Hormel Foods, LLC

Lawry's® Foods

© Mars, Incorporated 2006

MASTERFOODS USA

McIlhenny Company (TABASCO® brand Pepper Sauce)

National Honey Board

Nestlé USA

Ortega®, A Division of B&G Foods, Inc.

Reckitt Benckiser Inc.

Sargento® Foods Inc.

Sonoma® Dried Tomatoes

Unilever Foods North America

Washington Apple Commission

Wisconsin Milk Marketing Board

Index

METRIC CONVERSION CHART

VOLUME MEASUREMENTS (dry)

1/8 teaspoon = 0.5 mL
1/4 teaspoon = 1 mL
1/2 teaspoon = 2 mL
3/4 teaspoon = 4 mL
1 teaspoon = 5 mL
1 tablespoon = 15 mL
2 tablespoons = 30 mL
1/4 cup = 60 mL
1/3 cup = 75 mL
1/2 cup = 125 mL
2/3 cup = 150 mL
3/4 cup = 175 mL
1 cup = 250 mL
2 cups = 1 pint = 500 mL
3 cups = 750 mL
4 cups = 1 quart = 1 L

VOLUME MEASUREMENTS (fluid)

1 fluid ounce (2 tablespoons) = 30 mL
4 fluid ounces (1/2 cup) = 125 mL
8 fluid ounces (1 cup) = 250 mL
12 fluid ounces (1 1/2 cups) = 375 mL
16 fluid ounces (2 cups) = 500 mL

WEIGHTS (mass)

1/2 ounce = 15 g
1 ounce = 30 g
3 ounces = 90 g
4 ounces = 120 g
8 ounces = 225 g
10 ounces = 285 g
12 ounces = 360 g
16 ounces = 1 pound = 450 g

DIMENSIONS

1/16 inch = 2 mm
1/8 inch = 3 mm
1/4 inch = 6 mm
1/2 inch = 1.5 cm
3/4 inch = 2 cm
1 inch = 2.5 cm

OVEN TEMPERATURES

250°F = 120°C
275°F = 140°C
300°F = 150°C
325°F = 160°C
350°F = 180°C
375°F = 190°C
400°F = 200°C
425°F = 220°C
450°F = 230°C

BAKING PAN SIZES

Utensil	Size in Inches/Quarts	Metric Volume	Size in Centimeters
Baking or Cake Pan (square or rectangular)	8×8×2	2 L	20×20×5
	9×9×2	2.5 L	23×23×5
	12×8×2	3 L	30×20×5
	13×9×2	3.5 L	33×23×5
Loaf Pan	8×4×3	1.5 L	20×10×7
	9×5×3	2 L	23×13×7
Round Layer Cake Pan	8×1½	1.2 L	20×4
	9×1½	1.5 L	23×4
Pie Plate	8×1¼	750 mL	20×3
	9×1¼	1 L	23×3
Baking Dish or Casserole	1 quart	1 L	—
	1½ quart	1.5 L	—
	2 quart	2 L	—

Metric Chart